# An Introduction to Literary Studies

Mario Klarer

LONDON AND NEW YORK

*For Bernadette, Johanna and Moritz*

Published 1998 (3rd revised edition) by
Wissenschaftliche Buchgesellschaft,
Darmstadt as *Einführung in die
anglistisch–amerikanistische
Literaturwissenschaft*
© 1998 Wissenschaftliche
Buchgesellschaft, Darmstadt

First published in English 1999
by Routledge
11 New Fetter Lane, London
EC4P 4EE

Simultaneously published in the USA
and Canada
by Routledge
29 West 35th Street, New York,
NY 10001

*Routledge is an imprint of the Taylor & Francis
Group*

© 1999 Routledge

Typeset in Baskerville and Frutiger by
The Florence Group, Stoodleigh, Devon
Printed and bound in Great Britain by
Clays Ltd, St Ives plc

*British Library Cataloguing in Publication
Data*
A catalogue record for this book is
available from the British Library

*Library of Congress Cataloging in Publication
Data*
Klarer, Mario, 1962–
   [Einführung in die anglistisch-
amerikanistische Literaturwissenschaft.
English]
   An introduction to literary studies/
Mario Klarer.
      p.  cm.
   Includes bibliographical references
and index.
      1. English literature—History and
criticism—Theory, etc.  2. American
literature—History and criticism—
Theory, etc.   I. Title.
   PR21.K5213   1999
   820.9—dc21                          99–25771
                                            CIP

ISBN 0–415–21169–7 (hbk)
ISBN 0–415–21170–0 (pbk)

# Contents

# Preliminary remarks

This concise introduction provides a general survey of various aspects of textual studies for college students who intend to specialize in English or American literature and want to acquire a basic familiarity with the entire field. The book targets both the European and American college market: it is not only designed for beginners in the European system, where students have to specialize in one or two disciplines upon entering university, but it also meets the requirements for American undergraduates who have opted for a major in English and need an introduction to the more scholarly aspects of literary studies, one which goes beyond freshman Introduction to Literature courses. It therefore serves as a textbook for Introduction to English Literature classes at all major European universities or advanced undergraduate English (honors) courses in the USA and as an independent study guide. Its simple language and accessible style make the book equally apt for English native speakers as well as students of English Literature whose native language is other than English.

Unlike most of the existing American textbooks geared toward freshman Introduction to Literature courses, which emphasize the first-hand reading of primary texts, this book targets a slightly more advanced audience interested in the scholarly aspects of literature. The book does not include entire literary texts, but rather draws on a number of very short excerpts to illustrate major issues of literary studies as an academic discipline.

*An Introduction* deals with questions concerning the nature of "literature" and "text," discusses the three major textual genres, as well as film and its terminology, gives an overview of the most impor-tant periods of Literatures in English, and raises issues of literary theory. A separate section explains basic research and composition techniques pertinent for the beginner. An extensive glossary of the major literary and cinematic terms gives easy and quick access to terminological information and also serves as a means to test one's knowledge when preparing for exams.

In order to meet the expectations of contemporary textual studies, major emphasis is placed on the accessibility of literary theory for beginners. All major schools and approaches, including the latest developments, are presented with reference to concrete textual exam-ples. Film is integrated as a fourth genre alongside fiction, poetry and drama to highlight the interdependence of literature and film in both artistic production and scholarly inquiry. The chapters on basic research and composition techniques explain today's standard compu-tational facilities such as the online use of the *MLA International Bibliography* as well as the most important rules of the *MLA Style Sheet* and guidelines for research papers.

The book owes a great deal to my interaction with students in the Introduction to Literature classes which I taught at the American Studies and Comparative Literature Departments of the University of Innsbruck. I also owe thanks for suggestions and critical comments to friends and colleagues, including Sonja Bahn, Gudrun M. Grabher, Monika Messner, Wolfgang Koch and Elliott Schreiber. Large parts of the book were written during an Erwin Schrödinger Fellowship at the *Getty Center for the History of Art and the Humanities* in Santa Monica from 1992 to 1994. The English translation was completed at the *National Humanities Center* in North Carolina during a Rockefeller Fellowship in 1995/96. I am particularly indebted to a number of friends for reading the manuscript. Monika Fludernik, J. Paul Hunter, Ulrich C. Knoepflmacher, Christian Mair, Steven Marcus and Devin Stewart have been very generous in their advice. My biggest thanks go to my companion Bernadette Rangger for critically discussing every chapter of the book from its earliest stages to its final version, for having been with me during all these years and for having made these years a wonderful time.

# Acknowledgments

'Stop All the Clocks' on p. 32 from *W.H. Auden: Collected Poems* by W.H. Auden, edited by Edward Mendelson. Copyright © 1940 and renewed 1968 by W.H. Auden. Reprinted by permission of Random House, Inc.

Part of 'In a Station of the Metro' on p. 35 by Ezra Pound, from *Personae*. Copyright © 1926 by Ezra Pound. Reprinted by permission of New Directions Publishing Corp.

'l(a' on p. 37 is reprinted from *Complete Poems 1904–1962*, by E.E. Cummings, edited by George J. Firmage, by permission of W.W. Norton. Copyright © 1991 by the Trustees for the E.E. Cummings Trust and George James Firmage.

# Chapter 1

# What is literature, what is a text?

Look up the term **literature** in any current encyclopedia and you will be struck by the vagueness of its usage as well as an inevitable lack of substance in the attempts to define it. In most cases, literature is referred to as the entirety of written expression, with the restriction that not every written document can be categorized as literature in the more exact sense of the word. The definitions, therefore, usually include additional adjectives such as "aesthetic" or "artistic" to distinguish literary works from texts of everyday use such as telephone books, newspapers, legal documents and scholarly writings.

Etymologically, the Latin word "litteratura" is derived from "littera" (letter), which is the smallest element of alphabetical writing. The word **text** is related to "textile" and can be translated as "fabric": just as single threads form a fabric, so words and sentences form a meaningful and coherent text. The origins of the two central terms are, therefore, not of great help in defining literature or text. It is more enlightening to look at literature or text as cultural and historical phenomena and to investigate the conditions of their production and reception.

Underlying literary production is certainly the human wish to leave behind a trace of oneself through creative expression, which will exist detached from the individual and, therefore, outlast its creator. The earliest manifestations of this creative wish are prehistoric paintings in caves, which hold "encoded" information in the form of visual signs. This visual component inevitably remains closely connected to literature throughout its various historical and social manifestations. In some periods, however, the pictorial dimension is pushed into the background and is hardly noticeable.

Not only the visual – writing is always pictorial – but also the acoustic element, the spoken word, is an integral part of literature, for the alphabet translates spoken words into signs. Before writing developed as a system of signs, whether pictographs or alphabets, "texts" were passed on orally. This predecessor of literary expression, called "oral poetry," consisted of texts stored in a bard's or minstrel's memory which could be recited upon demand. It is assumed that most of the early classical and Old English epics were produced in this tradition and only later preserved in written form. This oral component, which runs counter to the modern way of thinking about texts, has been revived in our century through the medium of radio and other sound carriers. Audio-literature and the lyrics of songs display the acoustic features of literary phenomena.

The visual in literary texts, as well as the oral dimension, has been pushed into the background in the course of history. While in the Middle Ages the visual component of writing was highly privileged in such forms as richly decorated handwritten manuscripts, the arrival of the modern age – along with the invention of the printing press – made the visual element disappear or reduced it to a few illustrations in the text. "Pure" writing became more and more stylized as an abstract medium devoid of traces of material or physical elements. The medieval union of word and picture, in which both components of the text formed a single, harmonious entity and even partly overlapped, slowly disappeared. This modern "iconoclasm" not only restricts the visual dimensions of texts but also sees writing as a medium which can function with little connection to the acoustic element of language.

It is only in drama that the union between the spoken word and visual expression survives in a traditional literary genre, although this feature is not always immediately noticeable. Drama, which is – traditionally and without hesitation – viewed as literature, combines the acoustic and the visual elements, which are usually classified as non-literary. Even more obviously than in drama, the symbiosis of word and image culminates in film. This young medium is particularly interesting for textual studies, since word and picture are recorded and, as in a book, can be looked up at any time. Methods of literary and textual criticism are, therefore, frequently applied to the cinema and acoustic media. Computer hypertexts and networks such as the *Internet* are the latest hybrids of the textual and various media; here writing is linked to sounds, pictures or even video clips within an interdependent network. Although the written medium is obviously the main concern in the study of literature or texts, this field of inquiry is also closely related to other media such as the stage, painting, film, music or even computer networks.

As a result of the permeation of modern textual studies with unusual media, there have been major controversies as to the definition of "text." Many authors and critics have deliberately left the traditional paths of literature, abandoning old textual forms in order to find new ways of literary expression and analysis. Visual and acoustic elements are being reintroduced into literature, and media, genres, text types and discourses are being mixed.

## 1 Genre, text type and discourse

Literary criticism, like biology, resorts to the concept of evolution or development and to criteria of classification to distinguish various genres. The former area is referred to as *literary history*, whereas the latter is termed *poetics*. Both fields are closely related to the issue at hand, as every attempt to define text or literature touches not only upon differences between genres but also upon the historical dimensions of these literary forms of expression.

The term **genre** usually refers to one of the three classical literary forms of *epic, drama,* or *poetry*. This categorization is slightly confusing as the epic occurs in verse, too, but is not classified as poetry. It is, in fact, a precursor of the modern novel (i.e., prose fiction) because of its structural features such as plot, character presentation and narrative perspective. Although this old classification is still in use, the tendency today is to abandon the term "epic" and introduce "prose," "fiction" or "prose fiction" for the relatively young literary forms of the novel and the short story.

Beside the genres which describe general areas of traditional literature, the term **text type** has been introduced, under the influence of linguistics. Texts which cannot be categorized under the canonical genres of fiction, drama and poetry are now often dealt with in modern linguistics. Scholars are looking at texts which were previously regarded as worthless or irrelevant for textual analysis. The term text type refers to highly conventional written documents such as instruction manuals, sermons, obituaries, advertising texts, catalogues, and scientific or scholarly writing. It can, of course, also include the three main literary genres and their sub-genres.

A further key term in theoretical treatises on literary phenomena is **discourse**. Like text type, it is used as a term for any kind of classifiable linguistic expression. It has become a useful denotation for various linguistic conventions referring to areas of content and theme; for instance, one may speak of male or female, political, sexual, economic, philosophical and historical discourse. The classifications for these forms of linguistic expression are based on levels of content, vocabulary, syntax, as well as stylistic and rhetorical elements. Whereas the term text type refers to written documents, discourse includes written and oral expression.

In sum, *genre* is applied primarily to the three classical forms of the literary tradition; *text type* is a broader term that is also applicable to "non-canonical" written texts, i.e., those which are traditionally not classified as literature. *Discourse* is the broadest term, referring to a variety of written and oral manifestations which share common thematic or structural features. The boundaries of these terms are not fixed and vary depending on the context in which they appear.

## 2   Primary and secondary sources

Traditional literary studies distinguish between the artistic object, or *primary source,* and its scholarly treatment in a critical text, or *secondary source.* **Primary sources** denote the traditional objects of analysis in literary criticism, including texts from all literary genres, such as fiction, poetry or drama.

The term **secondary source** applies to texts such as **articles** (or *essays*), *book reviews* and *notes* (brief comments on a very specific topic), all of which are published primarily in scholarly journals. In Anglo-American literary criticism, as in any other academic discipline, regularly published **journals** inform readers about the latest results of researchers (see Chapter 5). Essays are also published as **collections** (or *anthologies*) compiled by one or several editors on a specific theme. If such an anthology is published in honor of a famous researcher, it is often called a **festschrift**, a term which comes from the German but is also used in English. Book-length scholarly treatises on a single theme are called **monographs**. Most dissertations and scholarly books published by university presses belong to this group.

In terms of content, secondary literature tries to uphold those standards of scholarly practice which have, over time, been established for scientific discourse, including objectivity, documentation of sources and general validity. It is vital for any reader to be able to check and follow the arguments, results and statements of literary criticism. As the interpretation of texts always contains subjective traits, objective criteria or the general validity of the thesis can only be applied or maintained to a certain degree. This can be seen as the main difference between literary criticism and the natural sciences. At the same time, it is the basis for the tremendous creative potential of this academic field. With changes of perspective and varying methodological approaches, new results in the interpretation of texts can be suggested. As far as documentation of sources is concerned, however, the requirements in literary criticism are as strict as those of the natural sciences. The reader of a secondary source should be able to retrace every quotation or paraphrase (summary) to the primary or secondary source from which it has been taken. Although varying and subjective opinions on texts will remain, the scholarly documentation of the sources should permit the reader to refer back to the original texts and thus make it possible to compare results and judge the quality of the interpretation.

As a consequence of these conventions in documentation, a number of formal criteria have evolved in literary criticism which can be summarized by the term **critical apparatus**, which includes the following elements: *footnotes* or *endnotes*, providing comments on the main text or references to further secondary or primary sources; a *bibliography* (or *list of works cited*); and, possibly, an *index*. This documentation format has not always been followed in scholarly texts, but it has developed into a convention in the field over the last several centuries (see also Chapter 6).

| **forms of secondary sources** | **publishing media** |
|---|---|
| essay (article) | journal |
| note | anthology (collection) |
| book review | *festschrift* |
| review article | book |
| monograph | |

| **formal aspects of secondary literature** | **aspects of content** |
|---|---|
| footnotes | objectivity |
| bibliography | lucid arguments |
| index | general validity of |
| quotations | thesis |

The strict separation of primary from secondary sources is not always easy. The literary **essay** of the seventeenth and eighteenth centuries is a historical example which shows that our modern classification did not exist in rigid form in earlier periods. This popular genre treated a clearly defined, abstract or theoretical topic in overtly literary language, and thus possessed the stylistic features of primary sources; however, the themes and questions that it dealt with are typical for scholarly texts or secondary sources. From a modern perspective, therefore, the literary essay bridges two text types.

In the twentieth century, the traditional classification of primary and secondary sources is often deliberately neglected. A famous example from literature in English is T.S. Eliot's (1888–1965) modernist poem *The Waste Land* (1922), in which the American poet includes footnotes (a traditional element of secondary sources) in the primary text. In the second half of the twentieth century, this feature has been further developed and employed in two ways: elements of secondary sources are added to literary texts, and elements of primary sources – e.g., the absence of a critical apparatus or an overtly literary style – are incorporated in secondary texts. The strict separation of the two text types is therefore not always possible.

Vladimir Nabokov's (1899–1977) novel *Pale Fire* (1962) is an example of the deliberate confusion of text types in American literature. *Pale Fire* consists of parts – for instance, the text of a poem – which can be labeled as primary sources, but also of other parts which are normally characteristic of scholarly treatises or critical editions of texts, such as a "Foreword" by the editor of the poem, a "Commentary" with stylistic analysis as well as critical comments on the text, and an "Index" of the characters in the poem. In the (fictitious) foreword signed by the (fictitious) literary critic Charles Kinbote, Nabokov introduces a poem by the (fictitious) author Francis Shade. Nabokov's novel borrows the form of a *critical edition*, in which the traditional differentiation between literary text and scholarly commentary or interpretation remains clearly visible. In the case of *Pale Fire*, however, all text types are created by the author Vladimir Nabokov himself, who tries to point out the arbitrariness of this artificial categorization of primary and secondary sources. The fact that this text is named a novel, even though it has a poem at its center, calls attention to the relativity inherent in the traditional categorization of genres.

# Chapter 2

# Major genres in textual studies

As early as Greco-Roman antiquity, the classification of literary works into different genres has been a major concern of literary theory, which has since then produced a number of divergent and sometimes even contradictory categories. Among the various attempts to classify literature into genres, the triad *epic*, *drama*, and *poetry* has proved to be the most common in modern literary criticism. Because the epic was widely replaced by the new prose form of the novel in the eighteenth century, recent classifications prefer the terms *fiction*, *drama*, and *poetry* as designations of the three major literary genres. The following section will explain the basic characteristics of these literary genres as well as those of film, a fourth textual manifestation in the widest sense of the term. We will examine these types of texts with reference to concrete examples and introduce crucial textual terminology and methods of analysis helpful for understanding the respective genres.

## 1 Fiction

Although the novel emerged as the most important form of prose fiction in the eighteenth century, its precursors go back to the oldest texts of literary history. Homer's **epics**, the *Iliad* and the *Odyssey* (*c.* 7th century BC), and Virgil's (70–19 BC) *Aeneid* (*c.* 31–19 BC) influenced the major medieval epics such as Dante Alighieri's (1265–1321) Italian *Divina Commedia* (*Divine Comedy*; *c.* 1307–21) and the early modern English epics such as Edmund Spenser's (*c.* 1552–99) *Faerie Queene* (1590; 1596) and John Milton's (1608–74) baroque long poem *Paradise Lost* (1667). The majority of traditional epics center around a hero who has to fulfill a number of tasks of national or cosmic significance in a multiplicity of episodes. Classical epics in particular, through their roots in myth, history, and religion, reflect a self-contained worldview of their particular periods and nationalities. With the obliteration of a unified *Weltanschauung* in early modern times, the position of the epic weakened and it was eventually replaced by the novel, the mouthpiece of relativism that was emerging in all aspects of cultural discourse.

Although traditional epics are written in verse, they clearly distinguish themselves from other forms of poetry by length, narrative structure, depiction of characters, and plot patterns and are therefore regarded – together with the **romance** – as precursors of the modern novel. As early as classical times, but more strongly in the late Middle Ages, the romance established itself as an independent genre. Ancient romances such as Apuleius's *Golden Ass* (2nd century AD) were usually written in prose, while medieval works of this genre use verse forms, as in the anonymous Middle English Arthurian romance *Sir Gawain and the Green Knight* (fourteenth century). Despite its verse form and its eventful episodes, the romance is nevertheless considered a forerunner of the novel mainly because of its tendency toward a focused plot and unified point of view (see also the sections on plot and point of view in this chapter).

While the scope of the traditional epic is usually broad, the romance condenses the action and orients the plot toward a particular goal. At the same time, the protagonist or main character is depicted with more detail and greater care, thereby moving beyond the classical epic whose main character functions primarily as the embodiment of abstract heroic ideals. In the romances, individual traits, such as insecurity, weakness, or other facets of character come to the foreground, anticipating distinct aspects of the novel. The individualization of the protagonist, the deliberately perspectival point of view, and above all the linear plot structure, oriented toward a specific climax which no longer centers around national or cosmic problems, are among the crucial features that distinguish romance from epic poetry.

The **novel**, which emerged in Spain during the seventeenth century and in England during the eighteenth century, employs these elements in a very deliberate manner, although the early novels remain deeply rooted in the older genre of the epic. Miguel de Cervantes' (1547–1616) *Don Quixote* (1605; 1615), for instance, puts an end to the epic and to the *chivalric romance* by parodying their traditional elements (a lady who is not so deserving of adoration is courted by a not-so-noble knight who is involved in quite unheroic adventures). At the same time, however, Cervantes initiates a new and modified epic tradition. Similarly, the Englishman Henry Fielding (1707–54) characterizes his novel *Joseph Andrews* (1742) as a "comic romance" and "comic epic poem in prose," i.e., a parody and synthesis of existing genres. Also, in the plot structure of the early novel, which often tends to be episodic, elements of the epic survive in a new attire. In England, Daniel Defoe's (1660–1731) *Robinson Crusoe* (1719), Samuel Richardson's (1689–1761) *Pamela* (1740–41) and *Clarissa* (1748–49), Henry Fielding's *Tom Jones* (1749), and Laurence Sterne's (1713–68) *Tristram Shandy* (1759–67) mark the beginning of this new literary genre, which replaces the epic, thus becoming one of the most productive genres of modern literature.

The newly established novel is often characterized by the terms "realism" and "individualism," thereby summarizing some of the basic innovations of this new medium. While the traditional epic exhibited a cosmic and allegorical dimension, the modern novel distinguishes itself through grounding the plot in a distinct historical and geographical reality. The allegorical and typified epic hero metamorphoses into the protagonist of the novel, with individual and realistic character traits.

These features of the novel, which in their attention to individualism and realism reflect basic socio-historical tendencies of the eighteenth century, soon made the novel into a dominant literary genre. The novel thus mirrors the modern disregard for the collective spirit of the Middle Ages that heavily relied on allegory and symbolism. The rise of an educated middle class, the spread of the printing press, and a modified economic basis which allowed authors to pursue writing as an independent profession underlie these major shifts in eighteenth-century literary production. To this day, the novel still maintains its leading position as the genre which produces the most innovations in literature.

The term "novel," however, subsumes a number of subgenres such as the **picaresque novel**, which relates the experiences of a vagrant rogue (from the Spanish "picaro") in his conflict with the social norms of society. Structured as an episodic narrative, the picaresque novel tries to lay bare social injustice in a satirical way, as for example Hans Jacob Christoph von Grimmelshausen's (*c.* 1621–76) German *Simplizissimus* (1669), Daniel Defoe's *Moll Flanders* (1722) or Henry Fielding's *Tom Jones* (1749), which all display specific traits of this form of prose fiction. The **Bildungsroman** (novel of education), generally referred to by its German name, describes the development of a protagonist from childhood to maturity, including such examples as George Eliot's (1819–80) *Mill on the Floss* (1860), or more recently in Doris Lessing's (*1919) cycle *Children of Violence* (1952–69). Another important form is the **epistolary novel**, which uses letters as a means of first person narration, as for example Samuel Richardson's *Pamela* (1740–41) and *Clarissa* (1748–49). A further form is the **historical novel**, such as Sir Walter Scott's (1771–1832) *Waverly* (1814), whose actions take place within a realistic historical context. Related to the historical novel is a more recent trend often labeled **New Journalism**, which uses the genre of the novel to rework incidents based on real events, as exemplified by Truman Capote's (*1924) *In Cold Blood* (1966) or Norman Mailer's (*1923) *Armies of the Night* (1968). The **satirical novel**, such as Jonathan Swift's (1667–1745) *Gulliver's Travels* (1726) or Mark Twain's (1835–1910) *The Adventures of Huckleberry Finn* (1884), highlights weaknesses of society through the exaggeration of social conventions, whereas **utopian novels** or **science fiction novels** create alternative worlds with which to criticize real socio-political conditions, as in the classic *Nineteen Eighty-four* (1949) by George Orwell (1903–50) or more recently Margaret Atwood's (*1939) *The Handmaid's Tale* (1985). Very popular forms are the **gothic novel**, which includes such work as Bram Stoker's (1847–1912) *Dracula* (1897), and the **detective novel**, one of the best known of which is Agatha Christie's (1890–1976) *Murder on the Orient Express* (1934).

The **short story**, a concise form of prose fiction, has received less attention from literary scholars than the novel. As with the novel, the roots of the short story lie in antiquity and the Middle Ages. Story, myth, and fairy tale relate to the oldest types of textual manifestations, "texts" which were primarily orally transmitted. The term "tale" (from "to tell"), like the German "Sage" (from "sagen" – "to speak"), reflects this oral dimension inherent in short fiction. Even the Bible includes stories such as "Job" or "The Prodigal Son," (*c.* 4th–5th century BC) whose structures and narrative patterns resemble modern short stories. Other forerunners of this subgenre of fiction are ancient satire and the aforementioned romance.

Indirect precursors of the short story are medieval and early modern narrative cycles. The Arabian *Thousand and One Nights,* compiled in the fourteenth and subsequent centuries, Giovanni Boccaccio's (1313–75) Italian *Decamerone* (1349–51), and Geoffrey Chaucer's (*c.* 1343–1400) *Canterbury Tales* (*c.* 1387–1400) anticipate important features of modern short fiction. These cycles of tales are characterized by a frame-narrative – such as the pilgrimage to the tomb of Saint Thomas Becket in the *Canterbury Tales* – which unites a number of otherwise heterogeneous stories. On their way to Canterbury, the pilgrims tell different, rather self-contained tales which are only connected through Chaucer's use of a frame-story.

The short story emerged as a more or less independent text type at the end of the eighteenth century, parallel to the development of the novel and the newspaper. Regularly issued magazines of the nineteenth century exerted a major influence on the establishment of the short story by providing an ideal medium for the publication of this prose genre of limited volume. Forerunners of these journals are *The Tatler* (1709–11) and *The Spectator* (1711–12; 1714), published in England by Joseph Addison and Richard Steele, who tried to address the educated middle class in short literary texts and commentaries of general interest (essays). Even today, magazines like *The New Yorker* (since 1925) still function as privileged organs for first publications of short stories. Many of the early novels appeared as serial stories in these magazines before being published as independent books, for example, Charles Dickens' (1812–70) *The Pickwick Papers* (1836–37).

While the novel has always attracted the interest of literary theorists, the short story has never actually achieved the status held by book-length fiction. The short story, however, surfaces in comparative definitions of other prose genres such as the novel or its shorter variants, the novella and novelette. A crucial feature commonly identified with the short story is its impression of unity since it can be read – in contrast to the novel – in one sitting without interruption. Due to restrictions of length, the plot of the short story has to be highly selective, entailing an idiosyncratic temporal dimension that usually focuses on one central moment of action. The slow and gradual build-up of suspense in the novel must be accelerated in the short story by means of specific techniques. The short story's action therefore often commences close to the climax (*in medias res* – "the middle of the matter"), reconstructing the preceding context and plot development through flashbacks. Focusing on one main figure or location, the setting and the characters generally receive less detailed and careful depiction than in the novel. In contrast to the novel's generally descriptive style, the short story, for the simple reason of limited length, has to be more suggestive. While the novel experiments with various narrative perspectives, the short story usually chooses one particular point of view, relating the action through the eyes of one particular figure or narrator. The **novella** or **novelette**, such as Joseph Conrad's (1857–1924) *Heart of Darkness* (1902), holds an intermediary position between novel and short story, since its length and narratological elements cannot be strictly identified with either of the two genres.

As this juxtaposition of the main elements of the novel and the short story shows, attempts to explain the nature of these genres rely on different methodological approaches, such as reception theory with respect to reading without interruption, formalist notions for the analysis of plot structures, and contextual approaches for delineating their boundaries with other comparable genres. The terms plot, time, character, setting, narrative perspective, and style emerge not only in the definitions and characterizations of the genre of the novel, but also function as the most important areas of inquiry in film and drama. Since these aspects can be isolated most easily in prose fiction, they will be dealt with in greater detail in the following section by drawing on examples from novels and short stories. The most important elements are:

| | |
|---|---|
| Plot | (What happens?) |
| Characters | (Who acts?) |
| Narrative Perspective | (Who sees what?) |
| Setting | (Where and when do the events take place?) |

*a) Plot*

**Plot** is the logical interaction of the various thematic elements of a text which lead to a change of the original situation as presented at the outset of the narrative. An ideal traditional plot line encompasses the following four sequential levels:

exposition – complication – climax or turning point – resolution

The **exposition** or presentation of the initial situation is disturbed by a **complication** or *conflict* which produces suspense and eventually leads to a *climax, crisis,* or *turning point.* The **climax** is followed by a **resolution** of the complication (French *denouement*), with which the text usually ends. Most traditional fiction, drama, and film employ this basic plot structure, which is also called **linear plot** since its different elements follow a chronological order.

In many cases – even in linear plots – **flashback** and foreshadowing introduce information concerning the past or future into the narrative. The opening scene in Billy Wilder's (*1906) *Sunset Boulevard* (1950) is a famous example of the **foreshadowing** effect in film: the first person narrator posthumously relates the events that lead to his death while drifting dead in a swimming pool. The only break with a linear plot or chronological narrative is the anticipation of the film's ending – the death of its protagonist – thus eliminating suspense as an important element of plot. This technique directs the audience's attention to aspects of the film other than the outcome of the action (see also Chapter 2.4: Film).

The *drama of the absurd* and the *experimental novel* deliberately break with linear narrative structures while at the same time maintaining traditional elements of plot in modified ways. Many contemporary novels alter linear narrative structures by introducing elements of plot in an unorthodox sequence. Kurt Vonnegut's (*1922) postmodern novel *Slaughterhouse-Five* (1969) is a striking example of experimental plot structure which mixes various levels of action and time, such as the experiences of a young soldier in World War II, his life in America after the war, and a science-fiction-like dream-world in which the protagonist is kidnapped by an extra-terrestrial force. All three levels are juxtaposed as fragments by rendering the different settings as well as their internal sequences of action in a non-chronological way. Kurt Vonnegut offers an explanation of this complex plot structure in his protagonist's report on the unconventional literary practice of the extra-terrestrial people on the planet Tralfamadore:

> Tralfamadorian ... books were laid out – in brief clumps of symbols separated by stars ... each clump of symbols is a brief, urgent message – describing a situation, a scene. We Tralfamadorians read them all at once, not one after the other. There isn't any particular relationship between all the messages, except that the author has chosen them carefully, so that, when seen all at once, they produce an image of life that is beautiful and surprising and deep. There is no beginning, no middle, no end ... What we love in our books are the depths of many marvelous moments seen at one time.[1]

Kurt Vonnegut is actually talking about the structure of his own novel, which is composed of similarly fragmentary parts. The different levels of action and time converge in the mind of the protagonist as seemingly simultaneous presences. Vonnegut's technique of non-linear narrative, which introduces traditional elements of plot in an unconventional manner, conveys the schizophrenic mind of the protagonist through parallel presentations of different frames of experiences.

*Slaughterhouse-Five* borrows techniques from the visual arts, whose representational structures are considered to be different from literary practice. Literature is generally regarded as a temporal art since action develops in a temporal sequence of events. The visual arts, however, are often referred to as a spatial art since they are able to capture one particular segment of the action which can then be perceived in one instant by the viewer. Vonnegut and other experimental authors try to apply this pictorial structure to literary texts. Multi-perspectival narratives which abandon linear plots surface in various genres and media, including film and drama, always indirectly determining the other main elements, such as setting and character presentation.

### *b) Characters*

While formalist approaches to the study of literature traditionally focus on plot and narrative structure, methods informed by psycho-analysis shift the center of attention to the text's characters. A psychological approach is, however, merely one way of evaluating characters; it is also possible to analyze **character presentation** in the context of narratological structures. Generally speaking, **characters** in a text can be rendered either as types or as individuals. A typified character in literature is dominated by one specific trait and is referred to as a *flat character*. The term *round character* usually denotes a persona with more complex and differentiated features.

Typified characters often represent the general traits of a group of persons or abstract ideas. Medieval allegorical depictions of characters preferred **typification** in order to personify vices, virtues, or philosophical and religious positions. The Everyman-figure, a symbol of the sinful Christian, is a major example of this general pattern in the representation of man in medieval literature. In today's advertisements, typified character presentations re-emerge in magazines, posters, film and TV. The temporal and spatial limitations of advertising media revive allegorical and symbolic characterization for didactic and persuasive reasons comparable to those of the Middle Ages.

A good example of the purposeful use of typified character presentation occurs in the opening scene of Mark Twain's, "A True Story" (1874).

> It was summer-time, and twilight. We were sitting on the porch of the farmhouse, on the summit of the hill, and "Aunt Rachel" was sitting respectfully below our level, on the steps – for she was our servant, and colored. She was a mighty frame and stature; she was sixty years old, but her eye was undimmed and her strength unabated. She was a cheerful, hearty soul, and it was no more trouble for her to laugh than it is for a bird to sing . . . I said: "Aunt Rachel, how is it that you've lived sixty years and never had any trouble?" She stopped quaking: She paused, and there was a moment of silence. She turned her face over her shoulder toward me, and said, without even a smile in her voice. "Misto C—, is you inarnest?"[2]

The first paragraph of this short story provides a very formal configuration, where characters are reduced to mere types, yet still reflect a highly meaningful structure. The most significant constellation is rendered in one sentence: "'Aunt Rachel' was sitting respectfully below our level, on the steps – for she was our servant, and colored." The phrase "Misto C—, is you inarnest?" further specifies the inherent relationship. Twain manages not only to juxtapose African Americans and whites, slaves and slave-owners, but also female and male. In this very short passage, Twain delineates a formal relationship between two character types which also represents a multi-leveled structure of dependence. He introduces typified characterization for a number of reasons: as a stylistic feature of the short story which does not permit lengthy depictions, and as a meaningful frame within which the story evolves. The analyses of African American and feminist literary theory focus on mechanisms of race, class, and gender as analogously functioning dimensions. By juxtaposing a black, female slave with a white, male slave-owner, Twain highlights these patterns of oppression in their most extreme forms. The setting – a farm in the South of the United States – and, above all, the spatial positioning of the figures according to their social status (" 'Aunt Rachel' was sitting respectfully *below* our level, on the steps") emphasizes the mechanisms of dependence inherent in these mere character types.

The **individualization** of a character, however, has evolved into a main feature of the genre of the novel. Many modern fictional texts reflect a tension between these modes of representation by introducing both elements simultaneously. Herman Melville's (1819–91) novel *Moby Dick* (1851), for instance, combines allegorical and individualistic elements in the depiction of its main character in order to lend a universal dimension to the action which, despite being grounded in the particularities of a round figure, nevertheless points beyond the specific individual.

Both typified and individualized characters can be rendered in a text through *showing* and *telling* as two different **methods of presentation**. The **explanatory characterization**, or *telling*, describes a person through a narrator, for example, the depiction of Mr Rochester by the protagonist in Charlotte Brontë's (1816–55) novel *Jane Eyre* (1847).

> Mr. Rochester, as he sat in his damask-covered chair, looked different to what I had seen him look before; not quite so stern – much less gloomy. There was a smile on his lips, and his eyes sparkled, whether with wine or not, I am not sure; but I think it very probable. He was, in short, in his after dinner mood . . . [3]

In this example from a Victorian novel, the character is represented through the filter of a selective and judging narrator. This technique deliberately places the narrator in the foreground, inserting him or her as a judgmental mediator between the action and the reader (see the section on *point of view* in this chapter).

**Dramatic characterization**, or *showing*, does away with the position of an obvious narrator, thus avoiding any overt influence on the reader by a narrative mediator. This method of presentation creates the impression on the reader that he or she is able to perceive the acting figures without any intervening agency, as if witnessing a dramatic performance. The image of a person is "shown" solely through his or her actions and utterances without interfering commentary, thereby suggesting an "objective" perception which leaves interpretation and evaluation solely to the judgment of the reader. Ernest Hemingway's (1899–1961) texts are among the most famous for this technique, which aims at an "objective" effect by means of a drama-like presentation.

> "Will you have lime juice or lemon squash?" Macomber asked.
> "I'll have a gimlet," Robert Wilson told him.
> "I'll have a gimlet too. I need something," Macomber's wife said.
> "I suppose it's the thing to do," Macomber agreed. "Tell him to make three gimlets."[4]

This passage from "The Short Happy Life of Francis Macomber" (1938) exemplifies this technique, typical of Hemingway, which offers only the facade of his characters by dwelling solely on exterior aspects of dialogue and actions without further commentary or evaluation. Dramatic presentation, however, only pretends to represent objectively while it always necessarily remains biased and perspectival.

As shown above, one can distinguish between two basic kinds of characters (round or flat), as well as between two general modes of presentation (showing or telling):

**Kinds of characters**

| **typified character** | **individualized character** |
|---|---|
| flat | round |

**Modes of presentation**

| **explanatory method** | **dramatic method** |
|---|---|
| narration | dialogue – monologue |

Similar to typification and individualization, explanatory and dramatic methods hardly ever appear in their pure forms, but rather as hybrids of various degrees, since the narrator often also acts as a character in the text. Questions concerning character presentation are always connected with problems of narrative perspective and are therefore hard to isolate or deal with individually. The following section on point of view thus inevitably touches upon aspects already mentioned.

### c) Point of view

The term **point of view**, or narrative perspective, characterizes the way in which a text presents persons, events, and settings. The subtleties of narrative perspectives developed parallel to the emergence of the novel and can be reduced to three basic positions: the action of a text is either mediated through an exterior, unspecified narrator (*omniscient point of view*), through a person involved in the action (*first person narration*), or presented without additional commentary (*figural narrative situation*). This tripartite structure can only summarize the most extreme manifestations, which hardly ever occur in their pure form; individual literary works are usually hybrids combining elements of various types of narrative situations.[5]

The most common manifestations of narrative perspectives in prose fiction can, therefore, be structured according to the following pattern:

**omniscient point of view**
through external narrator who
refers to protagonist in the
third person

**first person narration**
by protagonist or
by minor character

**figural narrative situation**
through figures acting in
the text

Texts with an **omniscient point of view** refer to the acting figures in the third person and present the action from an all-knowing, God-like perspective. Sometimes the misleading term *third person narration* is also applied for this narrative situation. Such disembodiment of the narrative agent, which does away with a narrating persona, easily allows for changes in setting, time, and action, while simultaneously providing various items of information beyond the range and knowledge of the acting figures. Jane Austen (1775–1817), for example, introduces an omniscient narrator of this sort in her novel *Northanger Abbey* (1818):

> No one who had ever seen Catherine Moreland in her infancy, would have supposed her born to be a heroine. Her situation in life, the character of her father and mother, her own person and disposition, were equally against her. Her father was a clergyman, without being neglected, or poor, and a very respectable man, though his name was Richard – and he had never been handsome. He had a considerable independence, besides two good livings – and he was not in the least addicted to locking up his daughters. Her mother was a woman of useful plain sense, with a good temper, and, what is more remarkable, with a good constitution.[6]

As evident in this example, an omniscient narrator can go back in time ("Catherine Moreland in her infancy"), look into the future ("to be a heroine") and possess exact information about different figures of the novel ("Her situation in life ... Her father ... Her mother ... "). This omniscient point of view was particularly popular in the traditional epic but also widely used in the early novel.

**First person narration** renders the action as seen through a participating figure, who refers to her- or himself in the first person. First person narrations can adopt the point of view either of the protagonist or of a minor figure. The majority of novels in first person narration use, of course, the **protagonist** (main character) as narrator, as for example, in Laurence Sterne's (1713–68) *Tristram Shandy* (1759–67) or Charles Dickens' (1812–70) *David Copperfield* (1849–50). The opening lines of J.D. Salinger's (*1919) *The Catcher in the Rye* (1951) also refer to this tradition of first person narration by the protagonist. "If you really want to hear about it, the first thing you'll probably want to know is where I was born, and what my lousy childhood was like, and how my parents were occupied and all before they had me, and all that David Copperfield kind of crap, but I don't feel like going into it."[7] These first person narrations by protagonists aim at a supposedly authentic representation of the subjective experiences and feelings of the narrator.

This proximity to the protagonist can be avoided by introducing a **minor character** as first person narrator. By depicting events as seen through the eyes of another person, the character of the protagonist remains less transparent. A number of novels which center around a main figure, such as Herman Melville's (1819–91) *Moby Dick* (1851) or F. Scott Fitzgerald's (1896–1940) *The Great Gatsby* (1925), mystify the protagonist by using this particular technique. The opening words of *Moby Dick*, "Call me Ishmael," are uttered by the minor character Ishmael, who subsequently describes the mysterious protagonist Captain Ahab. In *The Great Gatsby*, Nick relates the events around the enigmatic Gatsby from the periphery of the action. Through this deliberately chosen narrative perspective, the author anticipates thematic aspects of the evolving plot.

In the **figural narrative situation**, the narrator moves into the background, suggesting that the plot is revealed solely through the actions of the characters in the text. This literary technique is a relatively recent phenomenon, one which has been developed with the rise of the modern novel, mostly in order to encourage the reader to judge the action without an intervening commentator. The following example from James Joyce's (1882–1941) *A Portrait of the Artist as a Young Man* (1916) renders the action through the figural perspective of the protagonist.

> The fellows had seen him running. They closed round him in a ring, pushing one against another to hear.
> – Tell us! Tell us!
> – What did he say? . . .
> He told them what he had said and what the rector had said and, when he had told them, all the fellows flung their caps spinning up into the air and cried:
> – Hurroo! . . .
> The cheers died away in the soft gray air. He was alone. He was happy and free.[8]

This example shows how a particular point of view can be rendered through different modes of presentation. In the above passage, direct speech and mental reflections are employed to reveal the action through the perspective of the protagonist. In contrast to an *omniscient point of view*, this form of third person narrative is bound to the perspective of a figure who is also part of the action.

If a text shifts the emphasis from exterior aspects of the plot to the inner world of a character, its narrative technique is usually referred to as **stream of consciousness technique**. Related narratological phenomena are *interior monologue* and *free indirect discourse*. The narrator disappears, leaving the thoughts and psychic reactions of a participating figure as the sole mediators of the action. Influenced by Sigmund Freud's psychoanalysis, this technique found its way into modernist prose fiction after World War I. Based on associations in the subconscious of a fictitious persona, it reflects a groundbreaking shift in cultural paradigms during the first decades of the twentieth century, when literature, under the influence of psychoanalysis and related sciences, shifted its main focus from the sociologically descriptive goals of the nineteenth century to psychic phenomena of the individual. James Joyce is considered the inventor of this technique, best exemplified by the final section of his novel *Ulysses* (1922), which strings together mental associations of the character Molly Bloom. A famous example in American literature is William Faulkner's (1897–1962) renderings of impressions and events through the inner perspective of a mentally handicapped character in *The Sound and the Fury* (1929). These experimental narrative techniques of character presentation became the major structural features of Modernism, thereby characterizing an entire literary era at the beginning of the twentieth century.

A good example is Virginia Woolf's (1882–1941) novel *Mrs Dalloway* (1925), which presents events not only through the thoughts of *one* person, but also through a number of other figures. As indicated by the title, the character Clarissa Dalloway is at the center of the novel, yet Virginia Woolf depicts her protagonist through the psyches of different personae. These figures cross paths with Clarissa Dalloway, reacting to her and thus revealing a new character trait of the protagonist. Through the interaction between the different mental reflections, as well as a number of other structural elements, the novel achieves a closed and unified form. It is a striking example of how the use of narrative perspective, character presentation, setting, and plot-structure can create an interdependent network of elements which work toward a common goal.

Modernist and postmodernist novels introduce these techniques in very overt ways, often even **changing narrative perspectives** within one text in order to highlight decisive shifts in the course of action or narrative. The Canadian novelist Margaret Atwood (*1939), for example, begins the first section of her novel *The Edible Woman* (1969) in first person narration by the protagonist. The second part is then rendered in a figural narrative situation in order to emphasize the general alienation of the main character. "Marian was sitting list-lessly at her desk. She was doodling on the pad for telephone messages. She drew an arrow with many intricate feathers, then a cross-hatch of intersecting lines. She was supposed to be working ... "[9] When Marian regains her identity at the end of the novel, Atwood also switches back to the original first person narration. "I was cleaning up the apartment. It had taken me two days to gather the strength to face it, but I had finally started. I had to go about it layer by layer" (ibid.: 289). Later on, Atwood even lets the protagonist reflect about these narratological changes when Marian says: "Now that I was thinking of myself in the first person singular again I found my own situation much more interesting" (ibid.: 290). Atwood's novel is an obvious example of how thematic aspects of a text, such as the protagonist's loss of identity, can be emphasized on a structural level by means of narratological techniques such as point of view.

### d) Setting

**Setting** is another aspect traditionally included in analyses of prose fiction, and it is relevant to discussions of other genres, too. The term "setting" denotes the location, historical period, and social surroundings in which the action of a text develops. In James Joyce's (1882–1941) *Ulysses* (1922), for example, the setting is clearly defined as Dublin 16 June 1904. In other cases, for example William

Shakespeare's (1564–1616) *Hamlet* (*c.* 1601), all we know is that the action takes place in medieval Denmark. Authors hardly ever choose a setting for its own sake, but rather embed a story in a particular context of time and place in order to support action, characters, and narrative perspective from an additional level.

In certain forms of prose fiction, such as the gothic novel, setting is one of the crucial elements of the genre as such. In the opening section of "The Fall of the House of Usher" (1840), Edgar Allan Poe (1809–49) gives a detailed description of the building in which the uncanny short story will evolve. Interestingly, Poe's setting, the House of Usher, indirectly resembles Roderik Usher, the main character of the narrative and lord of the house.

> I know not how it was – but, with the first glimpse of the building, a sense of insufferable gloom pervaded my spirit. . . . I looked upon the scene before me – upon the mere house, and the simple landscape features of the domain – upon the bleak walls – upon the vacant eye-like windows – upon a few rank sedges – and upon a few white trunks of decayed trees – with an utter depression of soul which I can compare to no earthly sensation . . . Perhaps the eye of a scrutinising observer might have discovered a barely perceptible fissure, which, extending from the roof of the building in front, made its way down the wall in a zigzag direction, until its way down became lost in the sullen waters of the tarn.[10]

The description of the facade of the house uses words such as "features," "eye-like," and "depression" which are reminiscent of the characterization of a human face. "White trunks of decayed trees" refers to the end of Roderik Usher's family tree – he will die without heirs, the last of his line. The crack in the front of the building mirrors the divided psyche of the lord of the house. At the end of the story, Poe juxtaposes the death of Usher with the collapse of the building, thereby creating an interdependence between setting, characters, and plot.

The modernist novel *Mrs Dalloway* (1925) by Virginia Woolf (1882–1941) also relies heavily on setting to unite the fragmentary narrative perspectives into a single framework. As mentioned above,

Woolf employs the mental reflections of a number of figures in her novel ultimately to characterize her protagonist, Mrs Dalloway. Only through her carefully chosen use of setting can Virginia Woolf create the impression that the different perspectives or thoughts of the characters occur simultaneously. A variety of indicators in the text specifically grounds all events at a particular time and in a certain location. The action is situated in the city of London, which provides the grid in which the various reflections of the characters are intricately interwoven with street names and well-known sights. Temporal references such as the tolling of Big Ben, a sky-writing plane, and the Prime Minister's car appear in a number of episodes and thereby characterize them as simultaneous events that occur within different sections in the general setting of the city of London. At the outset of the novel, Woolf introduces temporal and spatial elements into the setting (see the italicized phrases in the following passage) which will later re-surface in the perspectival narratives of the respective mental reflections of the characters.

> Mrs Dalloway said she would buy the flowers herself . . . For having lived in Westminster – how many years now? over twenty – one feels even in the midst of the traffic, or walking at night, Clarissa was positive, a particular hush, or solemnity; an indiscernible pause; a suspense (but that might be her heart, affected, they said, by influenza) before *Big Ben strikes*. There! Out it boomed. First a warning, musical; then the hour, irrevocable. The leaden Circles dissolved in the air. Such fools we are, she thought, crossing *Victoria Street* . . . in the triumph and the jingle and the strange high singing of some *aeroplane* overhead was what she loved; life; *London*; this moment of June. For it was the *middle of June*. The *War was over*.[11]

Virginia Woolf consciously borrows from the visual arts, attempting to integrate formal elements of cubism into literary practice. The simultaneous projection of different perspectives in the characterization of a figure is a central concern of cubist art, which also tries to represent an object as seen from a number of perspectives in space simultaneously.

This example once again highlights the fact that the various levels of fiction, including plot, setting, point of view and characters, tend to receive full meaning through their interaction with one another. In the interpretation of literary texts, it is therefore important to see these structural elements not as self-contained and isolated entities, but rather as interdependent elements whose full meaning is only revealed in the context of the other features and overall content of the text. Ideally, the structural analysis of these levels in literary texts should not stop at the mere description of these features, but rather show to what ends they are employed.

## 2 Poetry

**Poetry** is one of the oldest genres in literary history. Its earliest examples go back to ancient Greek literature. In spite of this long tradition, it is harder to define than any other genre. Poetry is closely related to the term "lyric," which derives etymologically from the Greek musical instrument "lyra" ("lyre" or "harp") and points to an origin in the sphere of music. In classical antiquity as well as in the Middle Ages, minstrels recited poetry, accompanied by the lyre or other musical instruments. The term "poetry," however, goes back to the Greek word "poieo" ("to make," "to produce"), indicating that the poet is the person who "makes" verse. Although etymology sheds light on some of the aspects of the lyric and the poetic, it cannot offer a satisfactory explanation of the phenomenon as such.

Most traditional attempts to define poetry juxtapose poetry with prose. The majority of these definitions are limited to characteristics such as verse, rhyme, and meter, which are traditionally regarded as the classical elements that distinguish poetry from prose. These criteria, however, cannot be applied to modern prose poetry or experimental poetry. Explanations of the genre which combine poetic language with linguistic elements other than rhyme and meter do more justice to non-traditional forms such as free verse or prose poems. These approaches examine as lyric phenomena the choice of words as well as the use of syntactic structures and rhetorical figures. Although these elements dominate in some forms of poetry, they also appear in drama or fiction. In spite of the difficulties associated with the definition of poetry, the above-mentioned hetero-geneous criteria outline the major qualities that are conventionally attributed to poetry.

The genre of poetry is often subdivided into the two major categories of *narrative* and *lyric poetry*. **Narrative poetry** includes genres such as the epic long poem, the romance and the ballad, which tell stories with clearly developed, structured plots (see Chapter 2.1: Fiction). The shorter **lyric poetry**, the focus of the following comments, is mainly concerned with one event, impression or idea.

Some of the precursors of modern poetry can be found in Old English *riddles* and *charms*. These cultic and magic texts, for example the following charm "Against a Wen", which is supposed to help to get rid of boils, seem strange today, but were common in that period.

> Wen, wen, little wen,
> here you must not build, here have no abode,
> but you must go north to the nearby hill
> where, poor wretch, you have a brother.
> He will lay a leaf at your head.
> Under the paw of the wolf, under the eagle's wing,
> under the claw of the eagle, may you ever decline!
> Shrink like coal on the hearth!
> Wizen like filth on the wall!
> Become as small as a grain of linseed,
> and far smaller than a hand-worm's hip-bone and so very small
> that you are at last nothing at all.[12]

These religious or magical charms form the beginning of many national literatures. It has already been mentioned in the discussion of the primordial roots of literature that the magical-cultic dimension contributed decisively to the preservation of texts in early cultural history.

The next step in poetic expression abandons these overtly cultic origins and uses music as a medium, as for example the Middle English anonymous "Cuckoo Song" (*c*. 1250), which could be accompanied by an instrument.

| Cuccu | Cuckoo |
|---|---|
| Summer is icumen in, | Summer has come, |
| Lhude sing, cuccu! | Sing loud, cuckoo! |
| Groweth sed and bloweth med | The seed grows and the meadow blossoms, |
| And springth the wode nu; | And the wood springs; |
| Sing cuccu! | Sing, cuckoo![13] |

In this Middle English example, the **onomatopoeia** (verbal imitation of natural sounds) of the cuckoo's calling is clearly audible. The acoustic dimension is a typical feature of poetry, one which continues in modern pop songs. Singers like Bob Dylan (*1941) are often counted among the poets of the late 1950s and 1960s because the lyrics of their songs are comparable with poems.

In the Old English period, ancient forms of poetry such as the **elegy**, which laments the death of a dear person, were newly adapted. Thomas Gray's (1716–71) "Elegy Written in a Country Church Yard" (1751) or Walt Whitman's (1819–92) "When Lilacs Last in the Dooryard Bloom'd" (1865–66) are examples from later periods. The **ode**, which was also known in classical antiquity, was revived in the Renaissance and used in the subsequent literary periods. As John Keats' (1795–1821) "Ode on a Grecian Urn" (1820) demonstrates, it consists of several stanzas with a serious, mostly classical theme. However, the most important English literary form with a consistent rhyming pattern is the **sonnet**, which, from the Renaissance onward, has been used in poetry primarily to deal with the theme of "worldly love" (see the section on "rhythmic-acoustic dimension" in this chapter).

Although some elements discussed in the chapter on fiction can also be applied to the analysis of poetry, there are, of course, idiosyncratic features associated with the genre of poetry in particular. The following elements are not restricted to poetry alone, but nevertheless stand at the center of attention in analyses of this genre.

An important and controversial term is "image" or **imagery**, which is pertinent to a number of divergent issues under discussion. The word itself can be traced back to the Latin "imago" ("picture") and refers to a predominantly visual component of a text which can, however, also include other sensory impressions. Imagery is often regarded as the most common manifestation of the "concrete" character of poetry. Even if an abstract theme is at the center of the poem, the poet still uses concrete imagery in order to make it more accessible. The concrete character of poetic language can be achieved on *lexical-thematic*, *visual*, and *rhythmic-acoustic* levels which reflect the most important elements in poetry:

**lexical-thematic dimension**
diction
rhetorical figures
theme

| **visual dimension** | **rhythmic-acoustic dimension** |
| --- | --- |
| stanzas | rhyme and meter |
| concrete poetry | onomatopoeia |

### a) Lexical-thematic dimension

The issue of the narrator, which has been dealt with in the context of *point of view* and *characters* in the treatment of fiction, is usually referred to in poetry with the terms "voice" or "speaker." As poetry is often regarded as a medium for the expression of subjective, personal events – an assumption which does not always correspond to the facts – the issue of the speaker is central in the analysis of poems. The question whether the speaker and the author are one and the same person is, of course, also relevant for fiction. In the novel and in the short story, however, a distinctive use of point of view techniques easily creates a distance between the narrator and the author.

In longer poetic forms, the narrative situation can be as complex as that of the novel or the short story. A good example is Samuel Taylor Coleridge's (1772–1834) **ballad** "The Rime of the Ancient Mariner" (1798). Here, a *frame narrative* in a figural narrative situation relates an incident in which a wedding guest is addressed by an uncanny mariner. "It is an ancyent Mariner, / And he stoppeth one of three" (1–2). The Mariner then recounts his adventures in a detailed *first person narration*. "Listen, Stranger! Storm and Wind, / A Wind and Tempest strong! / For days and weeks it play'd us freaks" (45–47). By placing the story of the "Mariner" within a *frame narrative*, Coleridge presents the plot of the ballad on two levels (frame narrative and actual plot) as well as in two narrative situations (figural and first person narration). The ballad assumes a position between the epic long forms and the lyric short forms. In spite of a well-developed plot and complex narrative perspective the ballad is, however, surpassed by the epic and the romance in size and complexity.

The use of poetic language, more than the use of complex narrative situations, distinguishes poetry from other literary genres. Concrete nouns and scenes are employed in order to achieve this particular effect. In his "Elegy Written in a Country Church Yard" (1751), which deals with human transitoriness, Thomas Gray (1716–71) uses concrete images such as a cemetery, the ringing of a bell, a farmer returning from tilling, darkness and tomb stones. Objects and expressive scenes are described in order to make the poem concrete, although the actual theme of transitoriness is abstract. An elegy by W.H. Auden (1907–73) uses a similar technique.

> Stop all the clocks, cut off the telephone,
> Prevent the dog from barking with a juicy bone,
> Silence the pianos and with a muffled drum
> Bring out the coffin, let the mourners come. . . .
>
> He was my North, my South, my East, my West,
> My working week and my Sunday rest,
> My noon, my midnight, my talk, my song;
> I thought that love would last for ever: I was wrong.
>
> The stars are not wanted now: put out every one;
> Pack up the moon and dismantle the sun;
> Pour away the ocean and sweep the wood;
> For nothing now can ever come to any good.[14]

As this 1936 poem shows, Auden consciously introduces concrete objects ("juicy bone," "sun") and everyday situations ("working week," "Sunday rest") in order to treat the theme of mourning on a level that is familiar to the reader and therefore emotionally loaded. In contrast to philosophical texts, which remain abstract in their expression, poetry tries to convey themes in a concrete language of *images*.

Images and concrete objects often serve the additional function of **symbols** if they refer to a meaning beyond the material object. A cross in Christian thinking is, for example, much more than two crossed wooden bars. The poet can either use a commonly known, *conventional symbol* or create his own *private symbol* which develops its symbolic function in its particular context. The albatross in Samuel Taylor Coleridge's (1772–1834) "The Rime of the Ancient Mariner" (1798), for example, is a private symbol. In the course of the poem, the murdered bird becomes a symbol of natural order which has been destroyed by man. It is only in the context of Coleridge's ballad that the albatross takes on this far-reaching symbolic meaning.

Further stylistic features include **rhetorical figures**, or figures of speech. These classified stylistic forms are characterized by their "non-literal" meanings. Rhetorical handbooks distinguish more than two hundred different figures, of which simile and metaphor are those most commonly used in poetry. A **simile** is a comparison between two different things which are connected by "like," "than," "as," or "compare," as in Robert Burns' (1759–96) poem "A Red, Red Rose" (1796):

> Oh, my love is like a red, red rose
> That's newly sprung in June;
> My love is like the melody
> That's sweetly played in tune. . . .

The equation of one thing with another without actual comparison is called **metaphor**. If Burns said "My love *is* a red, red rose", instead of "Oh, my love is *like* a red, red rose," the simile would be transformed into a metaphor. In his poem "Auguries of Innocence" (c. 1803), William Blake (1757–1827) uses a different metaphor in every stanza:

> To see a world in a grain of sand
> And a heaven in a wild flower,
> hold infinity in the palm of your hand
> and eternity in an hour.

A grain of sand is used as a metaphor for the world, a flower for the sky, and so on. In the metaphor and in the simile, two elements are juxtaposed: the *tenor* (the person, object or idea) to which the *vehicle* (or image) is equated or compared. In "Oh, my love is like a red, red rose," "my love" functions as the tenor and "red rose" as the vehicle. Rhetorical figures are widely used in poetry because they produce a "non-literal" meaning and reduce abstract or complex tenors to concrete vehicles, which again enhances the concrete character poetry ought to achieve.

The "concreteness" or closed form of poetry is often evoked in literary theory by calling the poem a "verbal icon" or "verbal picture." An often-quoted example is the poem "Ode on a Grecian Urn" (1820), in which the Romantic poet John Keats (1795–1821) describes a painted Greek vase. It is an example of the use of **imagery** to achieve a pictorial effect. In the detailed description of various pictorial scenes, the poem is equated with a vase and is thus supposed to become part of the closed, harmonious form of the artifact.

> Thou still unravished bride of quietness,
> Thou foster child of silence and slow time,
> Sylvan historian, who canst thus express
> A flowery tale more sweetly than our rhyme.

The line "Thou foster child of silence and slow time" indicates that on the vase – as in any work of plastic art – time stands still. People are thus able to overcome their own transitoriness – evoked through the urn as a container for the ashes of the dead – through artistic production. Even 2,000 years after the artist's death, the work of art has the same power it had at the time of its creation. The pictorial portrayal on the vase is juxtaposed and compared with the lines of the poem, "who canst thus express / A flowery tale more sweetly than our rhyme." In the last stanza Keats directly refers to the round, closed shape of the vase as a model for poetry:

O Attic shape! Fair attitude! with brede
Of marble men and maidens overwrought,
With forest branches and the trodden weed;
Thou, silent form, dost tease us out of thought
As doth eternity: Cold Pastoral!

The "silent form" of the Attic vase is the poem's dominant concrete image, one which is not used for its own sake but rather to refer beyond the object to the form of poetry as such. In the description of the visual images on the vase, pictorial art is juxtaposed with literature; the closed and self-contained structure of the vase becomes a model for poetry. The durability of the work of art is praised and contrasted with man's ephemeral existance. The image of the vase therefore serves a triple function: as a symbol for pictorial art, as a model for the form of poetry, and as a concrete object which refers to the abstract theme of transitoriness and eternal fame.

In the first two decades of the twentieth century, the movement of **imagism** continued this tradition of pictorial expression in poetry. The theoretical program of this literary "school," which is closely associated with the American poet Ezra Pound (1885–1972), focused on the "condensation" of poetry into powerful, essential images. The German word for poetry, "Dichtung," was considered to mean the same as the Latin "condensare" ("to condense"), thus fitting very well the imagists' preoccupation with the reduction of poetry to essential "pictures" or "images." According to Pound, poetry should achieve the utmost clarity of expression without the use of adornment. Pound voices this opinion in one of his manifestos (1913): "An 'Image' is that which presents an intellectual and emotional complex in an instant of time . . . It is better to present one Image in a lifetime than to produce voluminous works."[15] The following poem from 1916 is practical example of imagism:

IN A STATION OF THE METRO
The apparition of these faces in the crowd;
Petals on a wet, black bough.

This poem was preceded by several longer versions until Pound reduced it to three stanzas by using an expressionistic word-picture for the portrayal of the crowds in a metro station. He starts with the people in the darkness of the station and then equates them with "Petals on a wet, black bough" (see metaphor). By using a pictorial element which is at the same time a common theme in Chinese nature painting, Pound emphasizes the pictorial character of his poem.

Pound drew on the Japanese poetic form of *haiku* as examples of this "condensing" form of poetry. They, too, contain three lines and on a thematic level refer to times of the day or seasons. These Japanese short poems are usually rendered in Chinese characters, which are far more suitable than our alphabetical writing for conveying the pictorial-concrete dimension which fascinated the imagist poets. The Chinese pictogram, which combines writing and picture, greatly influenced the imagists, whose main occupation was to present pure verbal images to their readers. They intended to compensate for the lack of the pictorial dimension in alphabetical writing by condensing language as much as possible.

## b) Visual dimension

While imagery in traditional poetry revolves around a transformation of objects into language, concrete poetry takes a further step toward visual art, concentrating on the poem's shape or visual appearance. This movement, which was revived in the twentieth century, has a long tradition, reaching from classical antiquity to the Latin Middle Ages and on to seventeenth-century England. Among the best-known picture-poems of English literature are George Herbert's (1593–1633) "Easter Wings" (1633) and "The Altar" (1633).

As shown on the next page, Herbert's poem conveys a visual as well as a verbal image of an altar, which the poet has constructed from parts which have been given to him by God. The building blocks of the altar are the words, which Herbert assembles in the shape of an altar. Herbert thus places himself in the Christian tradition, in which existence begins with the word: "In the beginning was the word, and the word was with God, and the Word was God" (John 1.1). Herbert builds an altar out of words and, upon it, he offers to God the poem, i.e., the very words themselves.

### *The Altar*

A broken Altar, Lord, Thy servant rears,
Made of a heart and cemented with tears;
Whose parts are as Thy Hand did frame;
No workman's tool hath touched the same.

A    heart    alone
Is    such    a    stone,
As    nothing    but
Thy power doth cut.
Wherefore each part
Of my hard heart
Meets in this frame
To praise Thy frame
To praise Thy name,

That if I chance to hold my peace,
These stones to praise Thee may not cease.
Oh, let Thy blessed sacrifice be mine,
And sanctify this altar to be Thine.

The following concrete poem by E.E. Cummings (1894–1962) is a modern example of an abstract visual-verbal arrangement, which – despite its idiosyncrasies – works according to structural principles similar to those seen in George Herbert's text:

l(a

le
af
fa

ll

s)
one
l

iness

The text of the poem can be reconstructed as follows: "a leaf falls loneliness" or "l(a leaf falls)oneliness". E.E. Cummings uses a single leaf falling from a tree as a motif for loneliness, arranging the letters vertically instead of horizontally in order to trace the leaf's movement visually. In the act of reading, the eye can follow the course of the leaf from top to bottom and also from left to right and back. In one instance, this movement is underlined by an arrangement in the form of a cross. The technical term for this cross-like placement of words or letters is *chiasmus*, which derives from the Greek letter "chi" ("X"). Here, the chiasmus is formed by a cross-like arrangement of letters in two consecutive lines:

    af
    fa

This poem contains further visual elements which form an inter-dependent network with levels of content. The double "l" of the word "falls" is at the center of the poem. These letters can easily be read as two "I"s for the first person singular, thus underlining the fall from "two-someness" to loneliness. In "l-one-liness" only one "l" remains, or, as Cummings expresses it:

    one
    l

As these examples show, traditional and experimental poetry often work with the pictorial aspects of language and writing or aim at combining these aspects. Attempts to turn a poem into a quasi-material object can be achieved not only on a thematic level through the use of concrete nouns or scenes, but also on the visual level through a particular layout of letters, words or stanzas.

## c) Rhythmic-acoustic dimension

In order to achieve the concrete quality of poetic language, sound and tone are employed as elements with their own levels of meaning. By choosing certain words in a line or stanza, a poet can produce a

**sound** or tone which is directly related to the content of the statement. The acoustic element, like a poem's visual appearance in concrete poetry, can enhance the meaning of a poem. The following passage from Alexander Pope's (1688–1744) "Essay on Criticism" (1711) is a self-reflexive example of this technique:

> True ease in writing comes from art, not chance,
> As those move easiest who have learned to dance.
> 'Tis not enough no harshness gives offense,
> The sound must seem an echo to the sense:
> Soft is the strain when Zephyr gently blows,
> and the smooth stream in smoother numbers flows;
> But when loud surges slash the sounding shore,
> The hoarse, rough verse should like the torrent roar.
> (365–72)

In these lines, Pope points out that, in what he considers a good poem, content and sound harmonize and form a unity ("The sound must seem an echo to the sense"). In lines 5 and 6, he mentions the west wind (Zephyr) and suggests its natural sound through the deliberate choice of words whose sounds ("z," "ph," "w," "oo," "th") are reminiscent of a gentle breeze. In lines 7 and 8, the harsh noise of the sea breaking on the shore is imitated by words with less gentle sounds ("sh," "gh," "v," "rr"). This unifying principle of sound and sense is of course not a goal for every poet, and modern examples often work against this more traditional attitude toward unity.

**Meter** and rhyme (less often, rime) are further devices in the acoustic dimension of poetry which hold a dominant position in the analysis of poems, partly because they are relatively easy to objectify and measure. The smallest elements of meter are *syllables*, which can be either stressed or unstressed. According to the sequence of stressed and unstressed syllables, it is possible to distinguish between various metrical *feet*, whose number consequently indicates the *meter*. In the analysis of the meter (scansion), a line is first divided into syllables. The example here is the verse "The woods are lovely, dark and deep" from Robert Frost's (1874–1963) poem "Stopping by the Woods on a Snowy Evening" (1923):

The – woods – are – love – ly, – dark – and – deep

After the division into syllables, **stressed** syllables (´) and **unstressed** syllables ( ˘ ) are identified. The technical term for this process is **scansion**:

Thĕ – woóds – ăre – lóve – lў, – dárk – ănd – deép

According to the sequence of stressed and unstressed syllables, the line can be divided into **feet**:

Thĕ – woóds | – ăre – lóve | – ly, – dárk | – ănd – deép.

The four most important feet are:

1 **Iambus**, or iambic foot: an unstressed syllable followed by a stressed syllable (˘´)
   Thĕ cúr | fĕw tólls | thĕ knéll | ŏf pár | tĭng dáy.
2 **Anapest**, or anapestic foot: two unstressed syllables followed by one stressed syllable (˘˘´)
   Ănd thĕ sheén | ŏf their spéars | wăs lĭke stárs | ŏn thĕ seá.
3 **Trochee**, or trochaic foot: a stressed syllable followed by an unstressed syllable (´˘)
   Thére thĕy | áre, mў | fíftў | mén ănd | wómĕn.
4 **Dactyl**, or dactylic foot: one stressed syllable followed by two unstressed syllables (´˘˘)
   Júst fŏr ă | hándfŭl ŏf | sílvĕr hĕ | léft ŭs.

According to the number of feet, it is possible to distinguish monometer (1), dimeter (2), trimeter (3), tetrameter (4), pentameter (5), and hexameter (6). In the description of the meter of a line, the name of the foot and the number of feet are mentioned. The first line of Thomas Gray's (1716–71) "Elegy Written in a Country Church Yard" (1751) ("Thĕ cúr | fĕw tólls | thĕ knéll | ŏf pár | tĭng dáy"), which consists of five iambic feet, is termed *iambic pentameter*. This meter, which is close to the rhythm of natural speech and therefore popular in poetry and drama, is also referred to as *blank verse*. Another popular meter in English is *iambic hexameter*, which is also called *Alexandrine*.

Alongside meter, **rhyme** adds to the dimension of sound and rhythm in a poem. It is possible to distinguish *internal, end* and *eye rhymes*. **Internal rhymes** are *alliteration* and *assonance*. **Alliteration** is the repetition of the same consonant at the beginning of words in a single line ("*r*ound and *r*ound the *r*ugged *r*ock the *r*agged *r*ascal *r*an"). If a vowel is repeated instead (either at the beginning or in the middle of words) it is called assonance ("Thou foster ch*i*ld of s*i*lence and slow t*i*me").

Alliteration was the most common rhyming pattern in Old English and in some types of Middle English poetry. The opening lines of William Langland's (*c.* 1330–86) Middle English "long poem" *Piers Plowman* (*c.* 1367–70) are good examples of a meter in which alliteration and stress complement each other.

> In a sómer séson, || whan sóft was the sónne
> I shópe me in shroúdes, || as Í a shépe were,
> In hábits like a héremite, || unhóly of wórkes
> Went wýde in this wórld, || wónders to hére.

In this meter, every line contains four stressed syllables with additional alliterations, while the number of unstressed syllables varies. In the middle, the line is split into two halves by a *caesura* which marks the beginning of a new unit of thought.

The most common rhyming scheme in modern poems is **end rhyme**, which is based on identical syllables at the end of certain lines. To describe rhyme schemes, letters of the alphabet are used to represent identical syllables at the ends of a line, as in the following poem by Emily Brontë (1818–48), "Remembrance" (1846):

> Cold in the earth – and in the deep snow piled above thee,   a
> Far, far removed, cold in the dreary grave!                  b
> Have I forgot, my only Love, to love thee,                   a
> Served at last by Time's all-severing wave?                  b

This system of identification helps to highlight the rhyme structure of complex poems by reducing them to their basic patterns.

**Eye rhymes** stand between the visual and the acoustic dimension of a poem, playing with the spelling and the pronunciation of words, as in these lines from Samuel Taylor Coleridge's (1772–1834) "Kubla Khan" (1816):

> Then reached the caverns measureless to man,
> And sank in tumult to a lifeless ocean:
> And 'mid this tumult Kubla heard from far
> Ancestral voices prophesying war!

The syllables "an" at the end of the first two lines are examples of eye rhyme, as the sequence of the letters "a" and "n" is identical, but pronounced differently in the two verses. Eye rhymes play with the reader's expectations. When reading the two lines in Coleridge's poem, one is tempted to pronounce the syllable "an" in "man" and "ocean" in such a way that the two words rhyme. By the time one gets to the word "ocean", however, it has become clear that they only rhyme visually and have to be pronounced differently. Eye rhymes permit authors to highlight certain words by creating a tension between visual and acoustic levels and thus to direct the reader's attention to specific elements of the poem.

The multitude of different **stanzas** in English poetry can be reduced to a few basic forms. Most poems are composed of *couplets* (two verses), *tercets* (three verses) or *quatrains* (four verses). The **sonnet** is an example of the combination of different stanzas. According to the rhyming scheme and the kind of stanzas, one can distinguish between *Shakespearean*, *Spenserian* and *Italian* (or *Petrarchan*) *sonnets*. In the Renaissance, sonnet cycles – consisting of a number of thematically related poems – became popular as a result of Italian influence. These cycles enabled poets to deal with certain topics in greater detail while working within the sonnet form.

The **English** or **Shakespearean sonnet**, which holds a privileged position in the English tradition, deserves a more detailed explanation. It consists of three quatrains and one couplet. The fourteen lines are in iambic pentameter and follow the rhyme scheme *abab cdcd efef gg*. Shakespeare's (1564–1616) sonnet "That time of year thou may'st in me behold" (1609) fulfills these criteria:

| | |
|---|---|
| That time of year thou may'st in me behold | a |
| When yellow leaves, or none, or few, do hang | b |
| Upon those boughs which shake against the cold, | a |
| Bared ruined choirs, where late the sweet birds sang. | b |
| In me thou see'st the twilight of such day | c |
| As after sunset fadeth in the west; | d |
| Which by-and-by black night doth take away, | c |
| Death's second self that seals up all in rest. | d |
| In me thou see'st the glowing of such fire | e |
| That on the ashes of his youth doth lie, | f |
| As the deathbed whereon it must expire, | e |
| Consumed with that which it was nourished by. | f |
| This thou perceiv'st, which makes thy love more strong, | g |
| To love that well which thou must leave ere long. | g |

Each segment of this sonnet (the three quatrains and the couplet) consists of a coherent sentence. The four sentences are connected on a thematic level by repetition: "in me behold" in the first verse, "In me thou see'st" in the fifth and the ninth, and "This thou perceiv'st" in the thirteenth. In each quatrain, an image is introduced which fits into the theme of the sonnet as a whole and works toward the couplet. In the first stanza, boughs without leaves are mentioned, followed by the setting sun and darkness in the second, and a dying fire in the third. Images from various areas all function as signs of mortality. In the couplet, a connection is drawn between these signs, which are visible in the speaker's face, and love. Indirectly, Shakespeare sees human love as arising out of the certainty of man's death. In this sonnet, the close connection between formal and thematic elements is clearly visible.

Ideally, in traditional poetry, the lexical-thematic, visual and rhythmical-acoustic dimensions – used here to illustrate the most important elements of the genre – should link with each other. The idea of unity, according to which several levels of expression connect, is most dominant in poetry, but, to a lesser degree, also characterizes other genres. One ought to be cautious, however, since not every poem subscribes to the concept of unity as its main structural goal. Experimental poetry, in particular, abandons these seemingly rigid structures in order to explore new "open forms," such as poems in prose or free verse.

## 3 Drama

So far we have identified distinct features belonging to *fiction* and *poetry*, two genres which rely on the written or spoken word as their primary means of expression. The dramatic or performing arts, however, combine the verbal with a number of non-verbal or optical-visual means, including stage, scenery, shifting of scenes, facial expressions, gestures, make-up, props and lighting. This emphasis is also reflected in the word **drama** itself, which derives from the Greek "draein" ("to do," "to act"), thereby referring to a performance or representation by actors.

Drama has its roots in cultic-ritual practice, some features of which were still present in stylized form in the classical Greek drama of the 5th century BC. Ancient tragedies and comedies were performed during festivals in honor of Dionysos, the god of wine. While drama was one of the main genres in classical antiquity, its importance waned with the dawning of the Middle Ages. After the turn of the millennium, however, simple forms of drama re-emerged. In **mystery** and **miracle plays**, religious, allegorical or biblical themes were adapted from Christian liturgy and dramatized for performance in front of churches and in the yards of inns. These medieval plays, together with the classical Roman plays by Plautus (*c.* 254–184 BC) and Seneca (*c.* 4 BC–65 AD), influenced later Renaissance drama, which reached its first peak in England with Shakespeare and his contemporaries.

While classical literary theory overlooks the nature of comedy, Aristotle (384–322 BC) deals extensively with the general elements and features of **tragedy**. In the sixth book of *The Poetics* he characterizes tragedy as "a representation of an action that is heroic and complete" and which "represents men in action and does not use narrative, and through pity and fear it effects relief."[16] By watching the tragic events on stage, the audience is meant to experience a **catharsis** or spiritual cleansing. **Comedy**, on the other hand, has humorous themes intended to entertain the audience. It is often regarded as the stylized continuation of primitive regeneration cults, such as the symbolic expulsion of winter by spring. This fertility symbolism culminates in the form of weddings, which comprise standard happy endings in traditional comedies.

Renaissance **history plays**, such as Shakespeare's (1564–1616) *Richard II* (1597) or *Henry IV* (*c.* 1597), adapt English history for stage performances. These plays portray a historical event or figure but, through the addition of contemporary references, transcend the historical dimension and make general statements about human weaknesses and virtues. In many cases, the author chooses a historical pretext in order to comment on contemporary socio-political misery while minimizing the risk of censorship.

William Shakespeare (1564–1616) and Christopher Marlowe (1564–93) revived and developed classical forms of drama such as tragedy and comedy and were among the first to reflect on different dramatic genres. A passage in Shakespeare's *Hamlet* (*c.* 1601) wittily testifies to this reflection: "The best actors in the world, either for tragedy, comedy, history, pastoral, pastoral-comical, historical-pastoral, tragical-historical, tragical-comical-historical-pastoral, scene individable, or poem unlimited" *(Hamlet*, II.2.378–81). Shakespeare parodies various mixed forms which, roughly speaking, can be reduced to the three basic forms of tragedy, comedy and history play.

When the Puritans under the rule of Oliver Cromwell and his Commonwealth (1649–60) shut down the English theaters on moral and religious grounds, drama lost its status as a major genre. Although religion exercised only a brief influence on drama in England in this drastic way (until the restoration of monarchy), it had far-reaching consequences in America. Because of the prominent position of Puritanism in American history, drama was almost nonexistent in the early phases of American literature and was only re-established as a serious genre in the beginning of the twentieth century.

During the Restoration Period in the late seventeenth century, the **comedy of manners**, or **Restoration Comedy**, portraying citizens from the upper echelons of society in witty dialogues, was very popular. William Congreve's (1670–1729) *The Way of the World* (1700) and William Wycherley's (1641–1715) *The Country Wife* (*c.* 1675) are well-known examples. The **heroic drama** of the time – such as John Dryden's (1631–1700) *All for Love* (1677) – tries to recreate and adapt epic themes on stage. In the Romantic period of the early nineteenth century, England produced the **closet drama**, a special form of drama which was not meant to be performed on stage but rather to be read in private. Percy Bysshe Shelley's (1792–1822) *Prometheus Unbound* (1820) is a well-known example of this unusual form of drama.

With the arrival of Realism and Naturalism in the late nineteenth century, social misery was dealt with on a broader scale and drama regained its importance as a major genre, albeit one which is intricately interwoven with developments in fiction (see Chapter 3). George Bernard Shaw (1856–1950) and Oscar Wilde (1854–1900) were among the most important playwrights of this period. All major developments in the theater of the twentieth century can be seen as reactions to this early movement, which favored a realistic representation of life. The Expressionist Theater and the Theater of the Absurd do away with the illusion that reality can be truthfully portrayed on stage, emphasizing more abstract and stylized modes of presentation. As with the postmodern novel, the parody of conventional forms and elements has become a striking feature in many plays of the second half of the twentieth century, such as Tom Stoppard's (*1937) *Travesties* (1974) and *Rosencrantz and Guildenstern Are Dead* (1966) or Samuel Beckett's (1906–89) *Waiting for Godot* (1952). Political Theater, characterized by social criticism, together with the movements which have already been mentioned, has become very influential. Important American examples are Clifford Odets' (1906–1963) Marxist workers' play *Waiting for Lefty* (1935) and Arthur Miller's (*1915) parable *The Crucible* (1953) about the political persecutions during the McCarthy era.

Because of the element of performance, drama generally transcends the textual dimension of the other two major literary genres, fiction and poetry. Although the written word serves as the basis of drama, it is, in the end, intended to be transformed into a performance before an audience. In order to do justice to this change of medium, we ought to consider *text, transformation* and *performance* as three interdependent levels of a play.

**text**
dialogue
monologue
plot
setting
stage directions

**transformation**
directing
stage
props
lighting

**performance**
actors
methods
facial expressions
gestures
language

*a) Text*

Since many textual areas of drama – character, plot and setting – overlap with aspects of fiction which have already been explained, the following sections will only deal with those elements specifically relevant to drama *per se*. Within the textual dimension of drama, the spoken word serves as the foundation for **dialogue** (verbal communication between two or more characters) and **monologue** (soliloquy). The **aside** is a special form of verbal communication on stage in which the actor "passes on" to the audience information which remains unknown to the rest of the characters in the play.

The basic elements of plot, including exposition, complication, climax, and denouement have already been explained in the context of fiction. They have their origin in classical descriptions of the ideal course of a play and were only later adopted for analyses of other genres. In connection with plot, the **three unities** of time, place and action are of primary significance. These unities prescribe that the time span of the action should be roughly the same as the duration of the play (or a day at the most) and that the place where the action unfolds should always be constant. Furthermore, the action should be consistent and have a linear plot (see Chapter 2.1: Fiction). The three unities, which were supposed to characterize the structure of a "good" play, have been falsely ascribed to Aristotle (384–322 BC). They are better identified for the most part as adaptations of his *Poetics* in the sixteenth and seventeenth centuries. These rigid rules for the presentation of time, setting and plot were designed to produce the greatest possible dramatic effect. Shakespeare's plays, which have always held a very prominent position in English literature, only very rarely conformed to these rules. This is why the three unities were never respected in English-speaking countries as much as they were elsewhere in Europe.

Indirectly related to the three unities is the division of a play into **acts** and **scenes**. Elizabethan Theater adopted this structure from classical antiquity, which divided the drama into five acts. In the nineteenth century, the number of acts in a play was reduced to four, and in the twentieth century generally to three. With the help of act and scene changes, the setting, time and action of a play can be altered, thereby allowing the traditional unity of place, time and action to be maintained within a scene or an act.

The Theater of the Absurd, like its counterpart in fiction, consciously does away with traditional plot structures and leads the spectator into complicated situations which often seem absurd or illogical. The complication often does not lead to a climax, resolution or a logical ending. In this manner, the Theater of the Absurd, like many postmodern novels or films, attempts artistically to portray the general feeling of uncertainty of the post-war era. Samuel Beckett (1906–89), whose play *Waiting for Godot* (1952) contributed to the fame of the Theater of the Absurd, is the best-known representative in the English-speaking world. Comparing Beckett's *Waiting for Godot* with a traditional plot, containing exposition, complication, climax and denouement, we find few similarities. The title of Beckett's play gives away the situation of the two main characters, Vladimir and Estragon; Godot himself receives no further characterization in the course of the play. The entrance of other characters briefly distracts from – but does not really change – the initial situation. The two main characters do not pass through the main stages of classical plot and do not undergo any development by the end of the play. Offering neither logical messages nor a conventional climax, Beckett's play consciously violates the expectations of audiences familiar only with traditional theater.

In the twentieth century, with the innovations of the Experimental Theater and the Theater of the Absurd, non-textual aspects of drama are brought to the foreground. Non-verbal features, which traditionally functioned as connecting devices between text and performance, abandon their supporting role and achieve an artistic status equal to that of the text.

### b) Transformation

**Transformation**, an important part of dramatic productions in the twentieth century, refers to the connecting phase between text and performance. It comprises all logistic and conceptual steps that precede the performance and are usually summarized under the heading **directing**. This transformation is not directly accessible to the audience; nevertheless, it influences almost all elements of the performance. The task of the contemporary director includes choosing the script or text, working out a general concept, casting, adapting the stage, selecting props, costumes and make-up and guiding the actors through rehearsals. The director is therefore responsible for the entire artistic coordination that guides the text into performance.

The profession of the director began to evolve in the late nineteenth century and is thus a relatively new phenomenon in the development of drama. Although directing, as a coordinating principle, is as old as drama itself, the lines separating the actors, authors and coordinators of a performance were, up to the nineteenth century, very vague. Every so often, the author himself would lead a production, or a more experienced actor would be given the task of directing. It was not until the second half of the nineteenth century that, with the development of Realism, the requirements of productions grew more demanding and the profession of the director was established as a mediator between authors and actors. Among the early directors, the Russian Konstantin Stanislavsky (1863–1938) is probably the most famous. His ideas and methods were adopted by the prestigious Lee Strasberg (1901–82) school of acting in New York and greatly influenced the American theater tradition. The Austrian director Max Reinhardt (1873–1943) also caused an uproar in the American theater world with some spectacular productions before World War I.

Since its earliest days as a profession, directing has been closely connected with all of the various movements in drama. In the beginning, directing centered mostly on realistic or historically authentic productions in which the director remained inconspicuous. In the twentieth century, the artistic fame of the director grew as a result of innovative ideas arising from Expressionist Theater, the Theater of the Absurd and Experimental Theater, which, together with the public's demand for an individual touch, increased the director's responsibility. With the focus shifting to production in modern drama, the director has moved from sidelines of the theater in the nineteenth century to the forefront, shaping a performance in his own unique style.

A good (dramatic) example of the importance of the director is demonstrated by Samuel Beckett's (1906–89) *Catastrophe* (1982), a short play with a comparatively large number of stage directions, whose self-reflexive subject is the production of a play. The highly stylized drama centers around a director, actor and helper who engage in the production of a performance. In this respect, *Catastrophe* is a highly postmodern work; the several levels of the play, including the transformation from text to performance, are already an integral part of Beckett's text, thereby laying bare the principles of drama *per se*.

Every step in the transformation of a text – the choice of the script, the accentuation of the play, the casting, the requirements of props, stage design, and rehearsal – has a specific audience in mind. What counts at this point is the director's conceptual idea. It resembles the interpretation of a score by a conductor, who emphasizes certain aspects of the "text" in order to convey an individual impression of a piece. This interpretive accentuation of a production is closely related to the trends of the time. For the success of productions like Ellis Rabb's (*1930) homoerotic interpretation (1970) of Shakespeare's *The Merchant of Venice* (*c.* 1596–98) or the many feminist adaptations of *The Taming of the Shrew* (*c.* 1592), the specific cultural and temporal conscience of the audience has to be considered. Productions need not necessarily be in tune with the obvious trends of the time to be successful – quite on the contrary, as proven by the productions of the American Robert Wilson (*1941), who borrows techniques from architecture and painting. Whatever the approach, the director needs to decide what kind of "tools" he is going to use in a production for a specific audience. All steps of the transformation – all verbal and non-verbal means of expression – are, ideally, included in the conceptual idea which runs like a thread through the entire production.

One of the aspects underlying every production is the spatial dimension. In traditional fiction, space is primarily expressed descriptively, whereas drama makes use of dialogue, monologue, body language, and above all the design of the stage, scenery, props and lighting for this purpose. Many elements of space are subject to historical conditions, but directors freely adapt older features for modern productions. The arrangement of the theater in a circle, for example, is an old concept dating back to ancient theater and is now being reused in modern productions to create a special interaction between the spectators and the actors.

The open-air structure of the classical **Greek amphitheater** included a space called *orchestra* in the center of the theater and a stage building, or *skene*. The seating was arranged in semi-circles around the orchestra. The actors could move between the skene and the orchestra while the chorus was positioned between the audience and the actors. In classical Greek drama, a mask was worn by every character or "person" – a term which can be traced back to the word "persona," meaning "mask."

**Elizabethan Theater** differs strongly from its classical precursors. A Greek theater could hold up to 15,000 spectators while an Elizabethan theater like the Globe could only contain a maximum of 2,000 people. The Globe Theatre in London was an octagonal building which had an uncovered courtyard with cheap seats. The more expensive seats were situated on three floors, in covered balconies that surrounded the inner courtyard. The stage stretched out into the courtyard on its lowest level, but also included an upper level which was directly adjacent to the balconies. In this manner, balcony scenes such as the one in *Romeo and Juliet* (1595) could be staged by making use of the lower and upper level of the stage. Because of the spatial separation of the stage areas, it was possible to stress thematic aspects of a play on a spatial level as well. In Shakespeare's *Richard II* (1597), for example, the submission of the king is not only highlighted in the dialogue but also visually and spatially as a change from an upper to a lower level: "Down, down I come, like glist'ring Phaeton . . . In the base court? Base court, where kings grow base" (*Richard II*, III.3. 178–80).

Elizabethan theater, like classical theater, worked without elaborate props. Many aspects which are depicted by scenery and other means in modern realistic drama were left to the spectator's imagination. Aspects of the setting which, from the Baroque onwards, were conveyed on a non-verbal level through painted scenery had to be expressed by the spoken word in Renaissance theater. In this manner, the dawning of a new day in *Romeo and Juliet* is expressed verbally: "The grey-eyed morn smiles on the frowning night, / Check'ring the eastern clouds with streaks of light; / And fleckéd darkness like a drunkard reels / From forth day's path and Titan's burning wheels" (*Romeo and Juliet*, II.3.1–4).

A parodistic example of verbal performance due to a lack of props can be found in the short "play within the play" in the last act of Shakespeare's *A Midsummer Night's Dream* (1595), in which amateur performers create a stage on the stage. In the "Prologue" to the performance, not only the characters of the play are introduced, but also the props, which in this scene are also represented by actors.

> This man with lime and roughcast doth present
> Wall, that vile Wall which did these lovers sunder;
> And through Wall's chink, pour souls, they are content
> To whisper. At the which let no man wonder.
> This man, with the lantern, dog, and bush of thorn,
> Presenteth Moonshine.

(V.1.130–5)

Shakespeare draws our attention here to the imaginary world which is created by the actors on stage, when these two actors "play" a wall in the moonshine. Shakespeare does more than merely parody the theater of his day – he also sheds light on the world of theater, showing it to be an illusion created by the interaction between actors, text and the imagination of the audience.

"Modern" theater, on the other hand, was characterized by an attempted realism which required stage, scenery and props to be redesigned. The stage took on the basic shape of a "box" with three walls and a ceiling, separating the audience from the actors more than in any of the preceding architectural shapes. Watching the performance on stage is like looking through an invisible fourth wall, the impression being one of a self-contained and independent world on stage. This **proscenium stage** was established in the eighteenth and nineteenth centuries and has remained the dominant form of stage design to this day. This new architectural shape of the theater is part of the development of Realism in literature, which stresses the importance of a supposedly truthful portrayal of reality. George Bernard Shaw's (1856–1950) plays are among the most important English contributions to this European movement. The plot of the drawing room comedy is an extreme example of the fusion of proscenium stage and realistic drama of that time. The play is staged in an almost authentic reconstruction of a drawing room and closely follows the three unities of place, time and action, as in Oscar Wilde's (1854–1900) *The Importance of Being Earnest* (1895). This tradition is continued in the twentieth century, as for example, in Eugene O'Neill's (1888–1953) *Long Day's Journey into Night* (c. 1941; published 1956), which is also designed for a drawing room setting.

In reaction to the realistic movement, there are a number of modern developments which, paralleling trends in poetry and prose, try to find new modes of presentation. **Expressionist Theater** in America was influenced by German Expressionist drama as well as by films and other art forms of the 1920s and 1930s. In drama, Expressionism is characterized by heavy, exaggerated make-up, costumes and settings. Elmer Rice's (1892–1967) *The Adding Machine* (1923) is an American example of the departure from the Realist-Naturalist theater. Rice uses expressionist elements to point out the estrangement of American city life, which is dominated by the alienating effect of an increasingly industrialized environment.

It is interesting that Expressionist Theater and the **Theater of the Absurd** both return to simple, abstract scenery and props. Expressionist make-up (which recreates the effect of the mask) and the empty stage of the Theater of the Absurd resemble older forms that were centered around the spoken word and the actor. In Samuel Beckett's (1906–89) *Waiting for Godot* (1952), the scenery consists merely of a park bench and a stylized tree; the stage design thus mirrors the emptiness of the dialogues. In Tom Stoppard's (*1937) *After Magritte* (1971), scenery and props are used in a slightly different way. On a non-verbal level of the play, the surrealist paintings of René Magritte (1898–1967), which are preoccupied with philosophical problems of language, are re-enacted on stage.

As many experimental pieces were not originally designed for performance in large established theaters, it was possible to experiment with stage forms. In particular, abandoning the traditional proscenium stage allowed for the discovery of new modes of interaction between actors and audience. The gap between stage and auditorium became less obvious and the audience could be included in the performance. In England, these experimental forms are referred to under the heading "Fringe Theatre," in America under "Off-Broadway" and "Off-Off-Broadway Theater," as they are not staged at the established theaters on Broadway.

As these examples show, the various elements of transformation and text influence each other. Plays designed for an unconventional stage generally differ from traditional plays in form and content. This fact indirectly affects the performance and requires special qualifications on the part of the actors.

### c) Performance

The last phase, the **performance**, centers around the actor, who conveys the combined intents of author and director. It has only been during the last hundred years that the methodological training of **actors** has established itself as a theatrical phenomenon alongside directing. Until the end of the nineteenth century, the transformation of the text was almost entirely in the hands of the actor. As the quality of acting in a play differed immensely between one performance and the next, methods had to be found that ensured constant results. Training in breathing, posture, body movements and psychological mechanisms facilitated the repeated reproduction of certain moods and attitudes on stage.

There are two basic theoretical approaches to modern acting: the external or technical method and the internal or realistic method. In the **external method**, the actor is supposed to be able to imitate the moods required in his part by using certain techniques, but without actually feeling these moods. The **internal method**, however, builds on individual identification of the actor with his part. Personal experience of feelings and the internalization of emotions and situations that are required in the part underlie the internal method. The external method relies on impersonation and simulation. It was impersonation, rather than internal identification with the role, that became the main goal of the school of acting in the United States under the Russian director Konstantin Stanislavsky (1863–1938), mentioned above, and his pupil Lee Strasberg (1901–82). This technique, known as *The Method*, stresses "showing" rather than "being." It has produced a number of famous actors such as Marlon Brando (\*1924), James Dean (1931–55), Paul Newman (\*1925) and Julie Harris (\*1925). Of the two approaches, method acting, with its emphasis on showing, is the one most widely applied in European theaters. Most of today's acting schools, however, borrow from both traditions, according to the requirements of the specific play to be performed.

Many aspects relating to figures in drama have already been discussed with regard to fiction. However, more than other genres, drama relies on acting characters (*dramatis personae*) and thereby gives rise to aspects that apply only to this genre. For instance, one cannot take for granted the interaction of several characters within a play. Originally, the **chorus** was the centerpiece of classical drama and only later were more characters added, creating the conditions for a dialogue between the figures and the chorus. The latter was originally a conveyor of lyrical poems which partly commented on the action of the play and partly addressed the actors in a didactic manner. The choir had a special status in Elizabethan theater, too, filling time gaps and informing the audience about new situations, as in Shakespeare's (1564–1616) *Henry V* (*c.* 1600). The terms "flat" and "round" for characters are as valid for drama as they are for fiction. Some types of drama, like comedy, have recurring character types, called **stock characters**, such as the boastful soldier, the cranky old man or the crafty servant.

As concerns gender, it is important to realize that in classical Greek theater as well as in Elizabethan theater women were banned from the stage, thus leaving all female roles to be played by young men. At times this led to complicated situations in comedies, as in Shakespeare's *As You Like It* (*c.* 1599), where female characters played by men suddenly dress up as men (cross-dressing). The female character Rosalind, who, according to the conventions of Elizabethan theater, was played by a young man, dresses up as a man in the course of the play. At the end of the play the character reveals her/his true female identity and marries Orlando. This tradition of casting men as women continued until the seventeenth century and was only abolished in Restoration drama.

Text, transformation and performance are central aspects not only of theater production; by analogy, they can also be applied to the medium of film, bearing in mind film's specific characteristics. Film-scripts differ from drama in that they take into account the visual, acoustic and spatial possibilities of the medium. Transformation in film is quite different from transformation in drama, which leads to a single, continuous performance. In film, only short sequences at a time are prepared for shooting, thus requiring that the actors work in ways which differ drastically from acting on stage. In theater, actors have to make themselves intelligible to the last row through heightened expression, exaggeration of facial expressions, gestures, make-up and voice projection. In film, these effects can be created through camera and sound techniques, giving the medium its specific quality and granting it the status of an independent genre, despite its strong connections with the traditional performing arts and its links with fiction's textual features.

## 4  Film

At the end of the twentieth century, it is impossible to neglect film as a semi-textual genre both influenced by and exerting influence on literature and literary criticism. Film is predetermined by literary techniques; conversely, literary practice developed particular features under the impact of film. Many of the dramatic forms in the twentieth century, for example, have evolved in interaction with film, whose means of photographic depiction far surpass the means of realistic portrayal in the theater. Drama could therefore abandon its claim to realism and develop other, more stylized or abstract forms of presentation. Photography and film have also had a major influence on the fine arts; novel, more abstract approaches to painting have been taken in response to these new media. The same can be said for postmodern fiction, which also derives some of its structural features from film.

Film's idiosyncratic modes of presentation – such as camera angle, editing, montage, slow and fast motion – often parallel features of literary texts or can be explained within a textual framework. Although film has its own specific characteristics and terminology, it is possible to analyze film by drawing on methods of literary criticism, as film criticism is closely related to the traditional approaches of textual studies. The most important of these methodologies coincide with the ones already discussed in connection with literary theory. There are, for example, approaches similar to text-oriented literary criticism which deal with material aspects of film, such as film stock, montage, editing, and sound. Methodologies which are informed by *reception aesthetics* focus on the effect on the spectator, and approaches such as psychoanalytical theory or feminist film theory regard film within a larger contextual framework. The major developments of literary theory have therefore also been borrowed or adapted by film studies.

In spite of their differing forms and media, drama and film are often categorized under the heading *performing arts* because they use actors as their major means of expression. The visualization of the action is not left merely to the imagination of a reader, but rather comes to life in the performance, independent of the audience. In both genres, a performance (in the sense of a visual representation by people) stands at the center of attention. It is misleading, however, to deal with film exclusively in the context of drama, since categorizing it under the performing arts does not do justice to the entire genre, which also includes non-narrative subgenres without performing actors.

The study of film has existed for quite some time now as an independent discipline, especially in the Anglo-American world. Since its invention a hundred years ago, film has also produced diverse cinematic genres and forms, which no longer permit a classification of film as a mere by-product of drama. Because of its visual power – the visual element plays only a secondary role in fiction – film is hastily classified as a dramatic genre. If film is dealt with from a formal-structuralist point of view, however, its affinity to the novel often overshadows its links to the play. Typical elements of the novel – varied narrative techniques, experimental structuring of the plot, foreshadowing and flashback, the change of setting and time structure – are commonly used in film. The stage offers only limited space for the realization of many of these techniques.

The most obvious difference between film and drama is the fact that a film is recorded and preserved rather than individually staged in the unique and unrepeatable manner of a theater performance. Films, and particularly video tapes, are like novels, which in theory can be repeatedly read, or viewed. In this sense, a play is an archaic work of art, placing the ideal of uniqueness on a pedestal. Every theatrical performance – involving a particular director, specific actors and scenery – is a unique event that eludes exact repetition. A film, on the other hand, can be shown in different cities at the same time, and it would be impossible to judge one screening as better or worse than any other one since the film always remains the same in its thousands of identical copies. In sum, one can say that although performance is at the heart of both drama and film, it takes on a completely different character in film, due to the idiosyncrasies of a mechanically reproducible medium.

The history of film in the nineteenth century is closely connected with that of photography. A quick succession of individual shots produces for the human eye the impression of a moving picture. To create this illusion, twenty-four pictures per second have to be connected. Within every second of a film, the motion of the projector is interrupted twenty-four times. Each picture appears on the screen for only a fraction of a second. The quick projections of images are too fast for the human eye, which does not pick up individual pictures, but rather sees a continuous motion. As early as the late nineteenth century, this physiological phenomenon was exploited to carry out the first successful cinematic experiments. In America, cinematic adaptations of narrative literature were carried out at the turn of the century. Among the first narrative films are children's stories such as Georges Méliès' (1861–1938) *Cinderella* (1899) or novels such as *Gulliver's Travels*

(Georges Méliès, 1901) and short stories such as *The Legend of Rip Van Winkle* (Georges Méliès, 1905). While the early films simply adopted the rigid perspective of the proscenium stage, the genre clearly departed from drama immediately prior to and during World War I. New techniques such as camera movement and editing were invented. An early American example in which these new techniques are applied is D.W. Griffith's (1875–1948) epic narrative film about the United States' rise to power, *The Birth of a Nation* (1915). Many of the major genres, such as the Western, slapstick comedies and love stories were already existent in the early American silent movie. Already by World War I, Hollywood had become the center of the film industry, with a widespread network of cinemas all over America.

Outside America, the Russian filmmaker Sergei Eisenstein (1898–1948) was one of the key figures in film history, inventing new techniques in the field of film editing in the years after the Russian Revolution. In Germany between the wars, Robert Wiene's (1881–1938) *Das Cabinett des Dr Caligari* (1919) and Fritz Lang's (1890–1976) *Metropolis* (1926) were famous contributions to Expressionist Film. Influenced by psychoanalysis, Expressionist Film added a new dimension to the medium, attempting, for example, to visualize dreams and other psychological phenomena.

When sound was introduced to film in the mid-1920s, some of the progressive visual techniques of the silent era were abandoned for a brief period in favor of sound and music. Because of the sheer weight of sound equipment, camera mobility was initially hampered. The acoustic dimension enabled the development of action through dialogues and not merely through the visual means of the preceding decades. By the 1930s, Hollywood's genres included the Western, the musical, gangster and adventure movies, science fiction, the horror film and opulent costume epics. After World War II, film noir ("dark film") developed as a new genre dealing with corruption in the disillusioned world of the American metropolis. Billy Wilder's (*1906) *Double Indemnity* (1944) and Robert Siodmak's (1900–73) *The Killers* (1946) are well-known examples.

In post-war Europe, the Italian Neo-Realist Film became internationally renowned through directors like Roberto Rosselini (1906–77), who treated realistic topics in authentic surroundings. In these films, the directors tried to capture the everyday life of post-war Italy by breaking away from the artificiality of the "closed" studio set and thereby founding novel cinematic forms. In the late 1960s, French directors such as Jean-Luc Godard (*1930) and François Truffaut (1932–84) gained international fame for their innovations in film. Through the Neuer Deutscher Film (*New German Cinema*), including the directors Rainer Werner Fassbinder (1946–82), Werner Herzog (*1942) and Wim Wenders (*1945), the German film enjoyed new international fame, which it had lost for some time. In the 1980s, young African American filmmakers were able to establish themselves alongside Hollywood directors. Spike Lee's (*1957) *Do the Right Thing* (1989) and John Singleton's (*1967) *Boyz N the Hood* (1991) are examples of a movement which in literary criticism had become known as "Minority" Literatures, including African American, Chicano, Gay and Lesbian self-expression.

In film, as in other genres, various levels contribute to the overall artistic impression. This medium, which strongly relies on technical aspects, has several important, uniquely cinematic features with their own terminology. The most essential elements of film can be subsumed under the dimensions of *space, time* and *sound.*

**spatial dimension**
film stock
lighting
camera angle
camera movement
point of view
editing
montage

**temporal dimension**
slow and fast motion
plot time
length of film
flashback
foreshadowing

**acoustic dimension**
dialogue
music
sound effects

### a) Spatial dimension

The deliberate choice of **film stock**, including black and white or color, high-contrast or low-contrast, sensitive or less sensitive material, produces effects which directly influence the contents of a film. The insertion of black and white material in a contemporary color movie, for example, can create the impression of a historical flashback. A similar effect can be achieved through the use of old newsreels from an earlier era of film. It is also possible to convey certain moods or to create specific settings by varying the choice of film stock. As early as 1939, Victor Fleming (1883–1949) used color-passages in *The Wizard of Oz* as a contrast to black and white film stock. Spike Lee (*1957) also inserts a short color passage into his black and white film *She's Gotta Have It* (1986) and thereby contrasts the feelings of the female protagonist in this particular scene with her other emotions, all of which are conveyed in black and white film stock.

**Lighting** is indirectly connected to film stock for certain light conditions have to be fulfilled according to the sensitivity of the film. A famous experiment in this respect is Stanley Kubrick's (*1928) film *Barry Lyndon* (1975) which uses only natural or candle light instead of electic light. Lighting is also used to obtain certain visual effects, as for example in Orson Welles' (1915–85) *Citizen Kane* (1941), where the director changes lighting parallel to the personal development of the protagonist, Charles F. Kane. While the young, idealistic Kane appears without shadows, later in the film his face is partially covered by shadows in order to point out the development of darker sides in his character.

Part of the spatial dimension is also the composition of the **frame**, whose elements are summarized under the French term *mis-en-scène*. **Mis-en-scène** literally means "to place on stage" and refers to the arrangement of all visual elements in a theater production. In film it is used as an umbrella term for the various elements that constitute the frame, including camera distance, camera angles, lenses, lighting, as well as the positioning of persons and objects in relation to each other.

Terms like *close-up*, *medium* and *long shot* refer to the distance of the camera from the object or to the choice of a particular section of

61

that object or person to be represented. With the aid of a long shot in a Western classic, a character almost completely vanishes in the landscape. The choice of this shot stresses vastness and human help-lessness in a wilderness where the character has to stand his ground. By using wide-angle lenses, similar effects can be achieved. Telephoto lenses create the opposite impression, either bringing the object closer to the foreground or making the background appear closer. A related technique is the use of distortions of the entire frame so that the image appears as if it were reflected in a curved mirror. A whole episode in Spike Lee's (*1957) *Crooklyn* (1994) uses a vertical distortion in order to make characters look like elongated Barbie dolls. Lee thereby evokes the experience of the child protagonist while visiting her relatives, whose worldview and role models are equally distorted.

An important consideration is the **camera angle** from which a certain scene is to be filmed. It is possible to distinguish between *high angle, straight-on angle* or *low angle shots* depending on the position of the camera. For example, if a character is supposed to appear tall, the camera is positioned low and aimed high *(low angle)*. In this manner, stylized distortions of size can be achieved. It is also possible to even out real misproportions. Actors like Humphrey Bogart (1899–1957) are filmed from a slightly lower angle so that they seem taller on screen than they are in reality. **Camera movement** is linked to camera angle and allows for a variable change of perspective. In the early days of film, the camera was too heavy to be moved during a scene. When lighter and more mobile equipment was developed, however, cameras began to move more freely.

The camera angle is closely related to issues of **point of view** in literature and poses similar questions. In the majority of films, the perspective is that of an omniscient "narrator" who at times borrows subjective points of view of characters in the film. In John Singleton's (*1967) *Higher Learning* (1995), for example, which is about race and gender prejudices, the camera at some points adopts the perspective and vision of a female protagonist. When this occurs, we as viewers of the film perceive – as if through the woman's eyes – the "male gaze" of men interested in her as a sexual object. Involuntarily, the viewer identifies with her and thus becomes aware of the effect a sexist gaze has on the person subjected to it. In a few rare cases, a subjective perspective or point of view is consistently maintained. In Robert Montgomery's (*1904) *Lady in the Lake* (1946) the entire plot, with only a few exceptions, is filmed from the perspective of the protagonist. The main character only becomes visible to the viewer when he looks into a mirror. This technique forces the viewer to identify with the protagonist, through whose eyes the action is seen.

**Editing** is one of the major cinematic techniques which have contributed to the flexibility of the medium. Already in Edwin S. Porter's (1870–1941) *The Great Train Robbery* (1903), the final version of the film was cut and rearranged in a separate process. The early Russian film developed **montage** as a filmic technique which creates effects similar to the use of the rhetorical figures of metaphor and simile in literature. Two pictures or objects that are in no way directly connected can be joined on a figurative level through montage. For example, in his film *Strike* (1924), Sergei Eisenstein (1898–1948) juxtaposes a massacre of workers with scenes from a slaughterhouse, thereby comparing the workers' fate with the slaughter of animals.

Most of the early cinematic experiments, using a rigid camera angle, simply adapted the setting of the proscenium stage. However, the technical innovations that followed enabled the medium to develop independently and led to the discovery of new forms of artistic expression. With the use of a mobile camera, editing, and montage, film definitely departs from its roots in the theater.

### b) Temporal dimension

Film, like literature, can employ the dimension of time in a variety of ways. Aspects of plot which have already been mentioned, such as *foreshadowing* and *flashback*, or interwoven levels of action and time, can be translated into film. The specific qualities of the medium enable the treatment of time in ways that do not exist in other genres. Simple examples of these techniques are fast-motion and slow-motion, which defamiliarize the action. In the film *Koyaanisqatsi* (1983), Godfrey Reggio (n.d.) uses fast-motion and slow-motion to draw attention to everyday situations such as city traffic or the changes of the seasons, stressing the importance of an ecological awareness on an endangered planet.

It is, however, not absolutely necessary to resort to special speeds in order to lengthen or shorten the temporal dimension. The cinema has other ways to create a discrepancy between the time span portrayed and the actual time. Stanley Kubrick's (1928–99) *2001: A Space Odyssey* (1968), for example, covers several million years of human evolution by cutting from a bone tool, thrown into the air by a caveman, to a futuristic spaceship. In the 1960 film version of the American short story "An Occurrence at Owl Creek Bridge" (1891) by Ambrose Bierce (1842–1914?) directed by Robert Enrico (*1931), just the opposite effect is created. A fraction of a second before the protagonist's death is expanded to about 30 minutes, the duration of the film. In his short story, too, Bierce had already experimented with objective time and time as experienced subjectively by the protagonist, who is being hanged on a railway bridge during the American Civil War. While the convict is falling, he imagines that the rope snaps and allows him to escape. What follows is the detailed description of his imaginary escape. The story ends abruptly with the death of the convict as his neck breaks. The reader realizes that the escape of the man took place entirely in his imagination, the duration of the scene encompassing only the interval between his fall and his death. In contrast to the above examples, films like Fred Zinnemann's (*1907) Western *High Noon* (1952) make the actual length of the film more or less correspond to the 90-minute time span of the action. The plot revolves around the elapsing time during which precautions are taken before a dangerous criminal arrives on the twelve o'clock (high noon) train. By equating real time and plot time, Zinnemann is able to emphasize the major feature of the film's content on a formal level, thus creating a powerful impression on the viewer.

The use of clocks, calendars, newspapers, signs of aging, or fashion are only some of the many ways to indicate the passage of time in film. In the discussion of character presentation and plot, the use of time indicators in Virginia Woolf's (1882–1941) novel *Mrs Dalloway* (1925) has already been pointed out. The novel consists of a number of simultaneously occurring episodes. Jim Jarmusch (*1953) uses a similar narrative technique in his film *Mystery Train* (1989), in which he presents the events in the lives of three groups of people in Memphis, Tennessee. The film is divided into three independent episodes which are connected by a number of time indicators. A revolver shot, a radio announcement and a passing train are recurring features in all three episodes, making it clear for the spectator that the episodes are taking place simultaneously. Like Virginia Woolf, Jarmusch here tries to present a picture from diverse, fragmented perspectives, which are nevertheless held together by a number of unifying elements. While *Mrs Dalloway* places the character of Clarissa at its center, *Mystery Train* revolves around the mystic figure of Elvis Presley, who is viewed from three different perspectives in three different episodes. As in Woolf's novel, multi-layered modes of character presentation are highlighted by complex narrative and temporal structures.

### c) Acoustic dimension

It was not until the 1920s that the acoustic aspect was added to film, bringing about a radical change of the medium. Information was no longer conveyed merely by means of visual effects such as facial expressions, gestures or subtitles, but also through language (dialogue or monologue), music and sound effects.

Billy Wilder (*1906) deals with the transition from silent film to sound film in *Sunset Boulevard* (1950). He plays with the concepts of verbal and non-verbal expression as the two basic dimensions of film. The two main characters – a script writer of the new sound film and a diva from the silent era – personify the discrepancies between "word" and "image." While the visual dimension of the medium is embodied by the diva, the acoustic dimension comes to life in the character of the script writer. In order to give an even sharper picture of the two underlying principles of verbal (dialogue) and non-verbal (facial expressions, gestures) communication, Wilder adds subjective commentary by the male protagonist which is built in as an interior monologue and acts as defamiliarizing element. Wilder's *Sunset Boulevard* is representative of a group of self-reflecting films concerned with the problems posed by the medium of film.

Beside dialogue and sound effects, film music assumes a special position and usually supports the plot. Volume, sound, rhythm and pace of the music change according to the situation and underscore levels of meaning with acoustic effects. Film music can also contrast with the plot and create ironic or parodistic effects. A good example is George Lucas' (*1944) *American Graffiti* (1973). In this portrayal of small-town American life from the point of view of young people, the music of the 1960s stands in sharp contrast to the plot. The youngsters are bored out of their minds as they cruise through town in their cars at night. The music from the loudspeakers of their car radios, laden with the typical themes of the American dream of freedom, fulfillment and love, creates an almost humorous effect, serving as a counterpoint to the actual disillusionment of the teenagers. Their reality is the monotonous recurrence of daily events, reflected in the circular movement of driving through the town.

Plot may be supported by the conventional and inconspicuous use of music and sound effects, or the action may be defamiliarized by contrasting the level of meaning and content with the acoustic level. In both cases, the acoustic dimension acts as an integral element of film, intricately interwoven with features of the spatial and temporal dimensions.

As with the individual elements treated in connection with the genres of fiction, poetry, and drama, the different dimensions of film can hardly be seen as self-contained entities. The isolation of elements is only a helpful tool for approaching a complex work of art and can never fully account for all of its interdependent subtleties. One must also be aware that the very act of differentiating levels and elements of a genre is inevitably arbitrary and always remains subject to current trends, methodological approaches, and the subjective preferences of the person who compiles them. The above dichotomies and classifications are, therefore, meant to facilitate first encounters with texts, but should by no means be taken as general patterns according to which texts must be interpreted. On the contrary, they should ideally yield to combinations with other suitable systems or eventually be selectively incorporated into one's personal methods of analysis.

# Chapter 3

# Periods of English Literatures

The following survey encompasses the most important movements of literatures written in English in their historical succession. In spite of many discrepancies and inconsistencies, some terms and criteria of classification have established themselves as standard in Anglo-American literary criticism. The convention of periodical classification must not distract from the fact that such criteria are relative and that any attempt to relate divergent texts – with regard to their structure, contents or date of publication – to a single period of literary history is always problematic. The criteria for classification derive from fields such as the history of the language (Old and Middle English), national history (Colonial Period), politics and religion (Elizabethan and Puritan Age) and art (Renaissance and Modernism). The following tables of the most important English and American literary periods provide a preliminary overview before they are dealt with individually.

## Periods of English Literature

| | |
|---|---|
| Old English Period | 5th–11th century |
| Middle English Period | 12th–15th century |
| Renaissance | 16th–17th century |
| Augustan Age | 18th century |
| Romantic Period | First half of 19th century |
| Victorian Age | Second half of 19th century |
| Modernism | First to Second World War |
| Postmodernism | 1960s and 1970s |

## Periods of American Literature

| | |
|---|---|
| Colonial or Puritan Age | 17th–18th century |
| Romantic Period and Transcendentalism | First half of 19th century |
| Realism and Naturalism | Second half of 19th century |
| Modernism | First to Second World War |
| Postmodernism | 1960s and 1970s |

The **Old English** or **Anglo-Saxon Period**, the earliest period of English literature, is regarded as beginning with the invasion of Britain by Germanic (Anglo-Saxon) tribes in the 5th century AD and lasting until the French invasion under William the Conqueror in 1066. The true beginnings of literature in England, however, are to be found in the Latin Middle Ages, when monasteries were the main institutions that preserved classical culture. Among the most important Latin literary texts is the *Ecclesiastical History of the English People* (731 AD) by Beda Venerabilis (672–735). As in other parts of Europe, national literatures developed in the vernacular parallel to the Latin literature. The earliest texts, written between the eighth and the eleventh centuries, are called Old English or "Anglo-Saxon." The number of texts which have been handed down from this period is very small, comprising anonymous magic charms, riddles and poems such as "The Seafarer" (*c.* 9th century) or "The Wanderer" (*c.* 9th–10th centuries), as well as several epic works such as the mythological *Beowulf* (*c.* 8th century) or *The Battle of Maldon* (*c.* 1000), which is based on historical facts.

When England was conquered by the French-speaking Normans in the eleventh century, a definite rupture occurred in culture and literature. From the later half of this **Middle English Period**, a number of texts from various literary genres have been preserved. The long list includes lyric poetry and epic "long poems" with religious contents, such as *Piers Plowman* (*c.* 1367–70), which has been attributed to William Langland (*c.* 1330–1386). The *romance*, a new genre of a secular kind, is developed in this period and includes the anonymous *Sir Gawain and the Green Knight* (fourteenth century) and Thomas Malory's (*c.* 1408–71) *Le Morte d'Arthur* (1470). This form indirectly influenced the development of the novel in the eighteenth century. Middle English literature also produced cycles of narratives, such as Geoffrey Chaucer's (*c.* 1340–1400) *Canterbury Tales* (*c.* 1387), similar to Giovanni Boccaccio's (1313–75) *Il Decamerone* (*c.* 1349–51) in Italy and comparable works of other national literatures, which are important models for the short story of the nineteenth century.

The **English Renaissance** is also called the Early New English Period, a term which focuses on the history of the language, and the Elizabethan Age (Queen Elizabeth I) or Jacobean Age (King James), divisions based on political rule. Particularly notable in this period is the revival of classical genres, such as the epic with Edmund Spenser's (*c.* 1552–99) *Faerie Queene* (1590; 1596), and the drama with William Shakespeare (1564–1616), Christopher Marlowe (1564–93) and others. Their revival of Greco-Roman genres was to influence and dominate the further course of English literary history. Besides the adaptation of drama and epic, the English Renaissance also produced relatively independent prose genres, as for example, John Lyly's (*c.* 1554–1606) romance *Euphues* (1578) or Philip Sidney's (1554–86) *Arcadia* (*c.* 1580). A quite unusual literary form showing affinity to drama of the time is the *Court Masque*, which relies on elaborate architectural designs. This period came to a close with the establishment of the Commonwealth (1649–60) under the guidance of the Puritan Oliver Cromwell. The prohibition of drama for religious reasons and the closure of public theaters during the "Puritan interregnum" greatly influenced English literary history. The outstanding literary *oeuvres* of this time were written by John Milton (1608–74), whose political pamphlets and religious epics (*Paradise Lost*, 1667 and

*Paradise Regained*, 1671) mark both the climax and the end of English Renaissance. In literary history the era after the Commonwealth is also referred to as the *Restoration* or sometimes – rather vaguely – as *Baroque*.

The next period which is commonly regarded as an independent epoch is the **Eighteenth Century**, which is also referred to as the *Neoclassical, Golden* or *Augustan Age*. In this period, classical literature and literary theory were adapted to suit contemporary culture. Authors such as John Dryden (1631–1700), Alexander Pope (1688–1744), Joseph Addison (1672–1719) and Jonathan Swift (1667–1745) wrote translations, theoretical essays and literary texts in a variety of genres. This was also a time of influential changes in the distribution of texts, including the development of the novel as a new genre and the introduction of newspapers and literary magazines such as *The Tatler* (1709–11) and *The Spectator* (1711–14). Daniel Defoe's (1660–1731) *Robinson Crusoe* (1719), Samuel Richardson's (1689–1761) *Pamela* (1740–41) and *Clarissa* (1748–49), Henry Fielding's (1707–54) *Tom Jones* (1749) and Laurence Sterne's (1713–68) *Tristram Shandy* (1767–68) marked the beginning of the novel as a new literary genre. It soon assumed the privileged position previously held by the epic or romance and became one of the most productive genres of modern literary history.

Much of the literary writing in America in the seventeenth and eighteenth centuries is religiously motivated and therefore may be subsumed under the rubric **Puritan** or **Colonial Age**. This period can be seen as the first literary phenomenon on the North American continent. Early American texts reflect, in their historiographic and theological orientation, the religious roots of American colonial times. Cotton Mather's (1663–1728) and John Winthrop's (1588–1649) notes in diary form and Anne Bradstreet's (*c.* 1612–72) poetry are among the most important sources for an understanding of the early colonies. In recent years there has been an increased interest in works by African American slaves, such as Phillis Wheatley's (*c.* 1753–84) *Poems on Various Subjects* (1773). These texts provide new outlooks on the social conditions of the period from a non-European perspective.

At the end of the eighteenth century, **Romanticism** marks the beginning of a new period in traditional English literary history. The first edition of the *Lyrical Ballads* (1798) by William Wordsworth (1770–1850) and Samuel Taylor Coleridge (1772–1834) is commonly considered to be the beginning of a new period in which Nature and individual, emotional experience play an important role. Romanticism may be seen as a reaction to the Enlightenment and political changes throughout Europe and America at the end of the eighteenth century. In addition to Wordsworth and Coleridge, the most important representatives of English Romanticism include William Blake (1757–1827), John Keats (1795–1821), Percy Bysshe Shelley (1792–1822) and Mary Shelley (1797–1851). In America, Romanticism and Transcendentalism more or less coincide.

Influenced by Romantic enthusiasm for nature and German Idealism, American **Transcendentalism** developed as an independent movement in the first half of the nineteenth century. Ralph Waldo Emerson's (1803–82) philosophical writings, including the essay *Nature* (1836), served as a foundation for a number of works which are still regarded as landmarks in the development of an independent American literary tradition. In Transcendentalism, nature provides the key to philosophical understanding. From this new perspective, man must not be satisfied with natural phenomena, but rather transcend them in order to gain a philosophically holistic vision of the world. Among the central texts of this movement, besides Ralph Waldo Emerson's philosophical writings, are Nathaniel Hawthorne's (1804–64) short stories, Henry David Thoreau's (1817–62) novel *Walden* (1854), Herman Melville's (1819–91) *Moby Dick* (1851), and Walt Whitman's (1819–92) poetry in *Leaves of Grass* (1855–92).

Subsequent to this period, America and England generally followed the course of the most important international literary movements. Toward the end of the nineteenth century, representatives of **Realism** and **Naturalism** can be found in both countries. Realism is often described as the movement which tries to truthfully describe "reality" through language. Naturalism, on the other hand, concentrates on the truthful portrayal of the determining effects of social and environmental influences on characters. While in the United States these trends manifest themselves mostly in fiction, England is also famous for its dramas of this period, including the works of George Bernard Shaw (1856–1950). American novelists such as Mark Twain

(1835–1910), Henry James (1843–1916) and Kate Chopin (1851–1904) and English authors such as Charles Dickens (1812–70), William M. Thackeray (1811–63), Charlotte (1816–55) and Emily Brontë (1818–48) and George Eliot (1819–80) are among the outstanding representatives of this era, which in England roughly coincides with the Victorian Age.

English and American **Modernism** can be seen as a reaction to the Realist movements of the late nineteenth century. While Realism and Naturalism focused on the truthful portrayal of reality, Modernism discovered innovative narrative techniques such as stream-of-consciousness or structural forms such as collage and literary Cubism. "Modernism" is a blanket term which encompasses the extensive literary innovations in the first decades of the twentieth century which manifest themselves under the influence of psychoanalysis and other cultural-historical phenomena. The main works include James Joyce's (1882–1941) *Ulysses* (1922) and *Finnegans Wake* (1939), Virginia Woolf's (1882–1941) *Mrs Dalloway* (1925) and *To the Lighthouse* (1927), Gertrude Stein's (1874–1946) *Three Lives* (1909), Ezra Pound's (1885–1972) *The Cantos* (1915–70), T.S. Eliot's (1888–1965) *The Waste Land* (1922) and William Faulkner's (1897–1962) *The Sound and the Fury* (1929).

In **Postmodernism**, modernist issues regarding innovative narrative techniques are taken up again and adapted in an academic, sometimes formalistic way. This literary movement of the second half of the twentieth century indirectly deals with Nazi crimes and the nuclear destruction of World War II while structurally developing the approaches of Modernism. Narrative techniques with multiple perspectives, interwoven strands of plot and experiments in typography characterize the texts of this era. Works such as John Barth's (*1930) *Lost in the Funhouse* (1968), Thomas Pynchon's (*1937) *The Crying of Lot 49* (1966), Raymond Federman's (*1928) *Double or Nothing* (1971) and John Fowles' (*1926) *The French Lieutenant's Woman* (1969) helped the movement to attain recognition in literary criticism. Both the Drama of the Absurd, including works such as Samuel Beckett's (1906–89) *Waiting for Godot* (1952) and Tom Stoppard's (*1937) *Travesties* (1974), and Postmodern film adapt many elements from Postmodern poetry and fiction to suit their media.

In the 1980s, the avant-garde works of Postmodernism, many of which seem exaggerated today, were overshadowed by Women's and **"Minority" Literatures**, that is literature written by marginalized groups including women, gays or ethnic minorities, the latter mostly represented by African Americans, Chicanos and Chicanas. These literatures, which have gained considerably in importance over the last few decades, sometimes return to more traditional narrative techniques and genres, often privileging socio-political messages over academic, structural playfulness. Writing by women, such as Sylvia Plath's (1932–63) *The Bell Jar* (1963), Doris Lessing's (*1919) *The Marriages Between Zones Three, Four and Five* (1980), Erica Jong's (*1942) *Fear of Flying* (1973) or Margaret Atwood's (*1939) *The Handmaid's Tale* (1985), and African American literature, including Richard Wright's (1908–60) *Native Son* (1940), Alice Walker's (*1944) *The Color Purple* (1980) and Toni Morrison's (*1931) *Beloved* (1987), or the works of Chinese-American authors such as Maxine Hong Kingston's (*1940) *The Woman Warrior* (1976) ensure the influential status of texts by women and minorities in contemporary literary criticism.

In addition to Women's Literature, **Postcolonial Literature** has recently become another center of attention. This vast body of texts is also categorized under *Commonwealth Literature, Literatures in English* or *Anglophone Literatures*. Literature from former British colonies of the Caribbean, Africa, India or Australia have contributed to a change in contemporary literature. In many cases – but by no means in all – dimensions of content have regained dominance and act to counterbalance the academic playfulness of Modernism and Postmodernism. Salman Rushdie's (*1947) *Satanic Verses* (1988), Derek Walcott's (*1930) *Omeros* (1990), Chinua Achebe's (*1930) *Things Fall Apart* (1958) and Janet Frame's (*1924) *An Angel at My Table* (1984) are respective examples of Anglophone literatures from Asia, the Caribbean, Africa and New Zealand. Partly under these influences the general trend seems to privilege less complicated and apparently more traditional narrative techniques, while at the same time focusing attention on content more than in earlier, exaggerated narrative forms.

This overview of the most important literary movements in English has only skimmed the surface of this wide and complex topic, leaving many authors unmentioned. Any survey in literary history confronts the issue of whether an exact classification of authors and their works is possible; such a classification must resort to conventions, in the absence of set guidelines. For this reason, authors like Aphra Behn (*c.* 1640–89), Edgar Allen Poe (1809–49), Ernest Hemingway (1899–1961) and John Steinbeck (1902–68) are not mentioned in this survey, since they cannot be assigned a definite place in this particular classification of periods and movements.

# Chapter 4

# **Theoretical approaches to literature**

As with the classification systems of genres and text types, the approaches to literary texts are characterized by a number of divergent methodologies. The following sections show that literary interpretations always reflect a particular institutional, cultural, and historical background. The various trends in textual studies are represented either by consecutive schools or parallel ones, which at times compete with each other. On the one hand, the various scholarly approaches to literary texts partly overlap; on the other, they differ in their theoretical foundations. The abundance of competing methods in contemporary literary criticism requires one to be familiar with at least the most important trends and their general approaches.

Historically speaking, the systematic analysis of texts developed in the magic and religious realm, and in legal discourse. At a very early date in cultural history, magic and religion indirectly furthered the preservation and interpretation of "texts" in the widest sense of the term. The interpretation of oracles and dreams forms the starting point of textual analysis and survives as the basic structures in the study of the holy texts of all major religions. The mechanisms at work are, however, most apparent in oracles. An ecstatic person (called a medium) in a state of trance received encoded information about future events from a divinity. These messages were often put into rhymed verse, which could preserve the exact words more easily than an oral prose text. Oral utterances could thus be "stored" through rhyme and meter in a quasi-textual way, making it possible to later retrieve the data in unchanged form. An important aspect of this oral precursor of written textual phenomena is that the wording of an utterance was seen as a fixed text that could consequently be interpreted. Famous classical examples of the different possible interpretations of oracles can be found in Herodotus' *Histories* (5th century BC).

The interpretation of encoded information in a text is important to all religions; it usually centers around the analysis or *exegesis* of canonical text such as the Bible, the Koran, or other holy books. As with dream and oracle, the texts which interpretations consequently decode are considered to originate from a divinity and are therefore highly privileged. It is important to observe that the interpretation of these kinds of texts deals with encoded information which can only be retrieved and made intelligible through exegetic practices. This religious and magical origin of textual studies can be traced from preliterate eras all the way to contemporary theology and has always exerted a major influence on literary studies.

Partly influenced by religion, legal discourse also had a decisive impact on textual studies. As with religious discourse, in law a fixed legal text had to precede jurisdiction. Juridical texts, like religious ones, are only indirectly accessible since by nature they demand interpretation with regard to a particular situation. The overall importance of legal texts in everyday life consequently led to an extensive body of literature concerning their application and interpretation. Even today, the exegesis of legal texts remains the form of interpretation most regularly confronted by the majority of people. Since most religions also include legal elements, such as Judaic Law, Islamic Law, or canon law in Christianity, religious and legal discourses have constantly coincided. The approaches and method-ologies associated with both (the exegesis of the Bible and the interpretation of legal texts) have always indirectly influenced literary studies.

Literary criticism derived its central term "interpretation" from these two areas of textual study. The *exegesis* of religious and legal texts was based on the assumption that the meaning of a text could only be retrieved through the act of interpretation. Biblical scholarship coined the term "hermeneutics" for this procedure, and it has been integrated into literary interpretation over the past several centuries. Since literary criticism as a discipline holds a variety of opinions – and, indeed, contradictory ones – concerning the purpose and applicability of textual interpretation, a number of theoretical trends and methodological approaches characterize the field.

Although each academic discipline tries to define and legitimate its scholarly work by terms like "general validity," "objectivity" and "truth," most disciplines are subject to a number of variable factors including ideologies, socio-political conditions and fashions. The humanities in general and literary studies in particular are character-ized by a multiplicity of approaches and methodologies. Within the field of literary studies, **literary theory** has developed as a distinct discipline influenced by philosophy. Literary theory analyzes the philo-sophical and methodological premises of literary criticism. While literary criticism is mostly interested in the analysis, interpretation and evaluation of primary sources, literary theory tries to shed light on the very methods used in these readings of primary texts. Literary theory thus functions as the theoretical and philosophical consciousness of textual studies, constantly reflecting on its own development and methodology.

Among the many diverse methods of interpretation it is possible to isolate four basic approaches which provide a grid according to which most schools or trends can be classified. Depending on the main focus of these major methodologies, one can distinguish between *text-, author-, reader-, and context-oriented approaches*. The following theo-retical schools can be subsumed under these four basic rubrics:

## Text
Philology
Rhetoric
Formalism and Structuralism
New Criticism
Semiotics and Deconstruction

## Author
Biographical Criticism
Psychoanalytic Criticism
Phenomenology

## Reader
Reception Theory
Reception History
Reader-Response Criticism

## Context
Literary History
Marxist Literary Theory
Feminist Literary Theory
New Historicism and Cultural Studies

The text-oriented approach is primarily concerned with questions of the "materiality" of texts, including editions of manuscripts, analyses of language and style and the formal structure of literary works. Author-oriented schools put the main emphasis on the author, trying to establish connections between the work of art and the biography of its creator. Reader-oriented approaches focus on the reception of texts by their audiences and the texts' general impact on the reading public. Contextual approaches try to place literary texts against the background of historical, social or political developments while at the same time attempting to classify texts according to genres as well as historical periods.

This classification inevitably results in a drastic reduction of highly complex theories to their most basic patterns. The following tries to depict the central tenets of these methodological approaches to texts, both as expressions of the cultural consciousness as well as of the ideologies of the era in which they exerted their major impact. This simplified categorization should not mislead the reader into believing that each theoretical school subscribes to a single, invariable methodology. Despite overlaps between many of the schools, each school's general outlook is dominated by one approach. The following survey is meant to highlight and summarize the main emphases of the most popular schools and theoretical trends in literary studies.

## 1  Text-oriented approaches

Many of the modern schools and methodologies in literary criticism adhere to **text-oriented approaches** and thereby indirectly continue to apply mechanisms rooted in the above mentioned primordial textual sciences of religion, legal practice, and divination. All these traditions place the main emphasis on the internal textual aspects of a literary work. Extra-textual factors concerning the author (his or her biography, other works), audiences (race, class, gender, age, education) or larger contexts (historical, social or political conditions) are deliberately excluded from the analysis. Although the text serves as the focal point of every interpretive method, some schools privilege other aspects such as biographical information concerning the author, problems of reception and the like which are only indirectly related to the literary work as such. Text-oriented traditions, however, center on the text *per se*, primarily investigating its formal or structural features. Traditional *Philology*, for example, highlights "material" elements of language, *Rhetoric* and *Stylistics* analyze larger structures of meaning or means of expression, and the Formalist-Structuralist Schools, including *Russian Formalism*, the *Prague School of Structuralism*, *New Criticism*, *Semiotics* and *Deconstruction*, attempt to trace general patterns in texts or illuminate the nature of "literariness."

### a) Philology

In literary criticism, the term **Philology** generally denotes approaches which center around editorial problems and the reconstruction of texts. Philology, which experienced its heyday in the Renaissance with the rediscovery of ancient authors, the invention of the printing press, and the desire for correct editions of texts, remained one of the dominant schools into the nineteenth century. Informed by the rise of modern science, these philological approaches tried to incorporate advanced empirical methodologies into the study of literature.

This positivist spirit is directly reflected in the major concordances (alphabetical lists of words) of nineteenth century literary scholarship, which document the exact frequency and usage of words by a particular author. These empirical studies not only list all words employed by Shakespeare in his dramas and poems, for example, but also provide the exact line reference for each entry. Concordances, as the most extreme developments of these positivist approaches in Philology, have been experiencing a revival due to current computer technologies. The possibility of transferring into electronic media large amounts of textual data such as the complete works of an author or all texts of an entire period (as for example the *Thesaurus Linguae Graecae*, which stores all written documents in ancient Greek on one CD-ROM), has given rise to computer-assisted frequency analyses of words and other similar quantitative or statistical investigations.

The materiality of texts, a major concern of traditional Philology, is still relevant to today's literary scholarship, as illustrated by the debate concerning the reliability of the generally accepted edition of James Joyce's (1882–1941) *Ulysses* (1922). In the 1980s, a number of competing Joyce editions, all of which considered themselves to be definitive texts, revived the interest in questions of textual editions and philological methodologies. These recent manifestations of traditional Philology, which sometimes focus on such arcane aspects as typography, are often referred to as *Textual Criticism*.

## b) Rhetoric and Stylistics

In addition to traditional editorial problems, today's text-oriented schools focus primarily on aspects of form (textual and narrative structure, point of view, plot-patterns) and style (rhetorical figures, choice of words or diction, syntax, meter). Together with Theology and Grammar, **Rhetoric** remained the dominant textual discipline for almost two thousand years. Since ancient Greco-Roman culture treasured public speech, Rhetoric compiled a number of rules and techniques for efficient composition and powerful oratory. Although Rhetoric was mainly concerned with teaching effectively how to influence the masses, it soon developed – as did the interpretation of holy and legal texts – into a theoretical academic discipline. In its attempt to classify systematically and investigate elements of human speech, Rhetoric laid the foundation for current linguistics and literary criticism.

Rhetoric originally mediated rules concerning eloquence and perfect speech and was hence primarily prescriptive. It offered guidelines for every phase of textual composition including *inventio* (selection of themes), *dispositio* (organization of material), *elocutio* (verbalization with the help of rhetorical figures), *memoria* (the technique of remembering the speech) and *actio* (delivery of the speech). Despite its prescriptive and practical inclination, Rhetoric also introduced descriptive and analytical elements into textual studies. Even in its earliest phases, Rhetoric analyzed concrete textual samples in order to delineate rules for the composition of a "perfect" text. In these theoretical investigations into textuality, structural and stylistic features – above all *dispositio* and *elocutio* – eventually surfaced as the most dominant areas of inquiry. Today's text-oriented literary criticism derives many of its fields from traditional Rhetoric and still draws on its terminology.

In the nineteenth century, Rhetoric eventually lost its influence and partially developed into **Stylistics**, a field whose methodology was adopted by literary criticism and art history as well. With the aim of describing stylistic idiosyncrasies of individual authors, entire nations, or whole periods, Stylistics focused on grammatical structures (lexis, syntax), acoustic elements (melody, rhyme, meter, rhythm) and overarching forms (rhetorical figures) in its analyses of texts. Although Stylistics experienced a slight revival a few decades ago, its main contribution to recent literary theory was as a precursor to formalist-structuralist schools of the twentieth century.

### c) Formalism and Structuralism

The terms **Formalism** and **Structuralism** encompass a number of schools in the first half of the twentieth century whose main goal lies in the explication of the formal and structural patterns of literary texts. This emphasis on the intrinsic and structural aspects of a literary work deliberately distinguished itself from older traditions – above all the biographical literary criticism of the nineteenth century – which were primarily concerned with extrinsic or extra-textual features in their analysis of literature. The consecutive schools of Russian Formalism, the Prague School of Structuralism, New Criticism and Poststructuralism find a common denominator – despite their respective idiosyncrasies – in their general attempts to explain levels of content in relation to formal and structural dimensions of texts.

In traditional philosophical and aesthetic discourse, *form* denotes the relationship between different elements within a specific system. Questions concerning form and content, already discussed by ancient philosophers, lie at the heart of this approach. According to this traditional point of view, things in the world only exist because shapeless matter receives structure through superimposed form. Form thus functions as a container in which content is presented. This basic philosophical principle, which distinguishes between a level of structure and a level of content, was introduced into literary criticism as early as classical antiquity. Aristotle (384–322 BC), for instance, in his *Poetics* (4th century BC) adopts the notion of the determining function of form over matter for literary phenomena by using formal schemes to explain generic features of drama. With this structural approach, Aristotle lays the basis for twentieth-century formalist movements in the study of literature and language. While a number of schools of literary criticism focus primarily on the level of content (the "what?" of a text), formalists and structuralists emphasize the level of form (the "how?" of a text).

During and after World War I, **Russian Formalism** sought an objective discourse of literary criticism by foregrounding structural analyses, or as Roman Jakobson (1896–1982) put it, "The subject of literary scholarship is not literature in its totality, but literariness, i.e., that which makes of a given work a work of literature."[17] In its search for the typical features of *literariness*, Russian Formalism rejects explanations which base their arguments on the spirit, intuition, imagination or genius of the poet. This "morphological" method developed by the formalists deliberately neglects historical, sociological, biographical or psychological dimensions of literary discourse, propagating instead an intrinsic approach which regards a work of art as an independent entity. In contrast to traditional, extrinsic methodologies, Russian Formalism privileges phonetic structures, rhythm, rhyme, meter, and sound as independent meaningful elements of literary discourse.

According to Victor Shklovski (1893–1984) and a number of other formalists, these structural elements in a literary text cause the effect called **defamiliarization**. This tendency inherent in literary language counteracts the reader's familiarity with everyday language and consequently offers a tool to distinguish between literary and non-literary discourse. Laurence Sterne's (1713–68) novel *Tristram Shandy* (1759–67), which abounds in a variety of defamiliarizations of its own genre, serves as the classic example in formalist explanations of these concepts. His novel starts much like a traditional autobiography which relates the life of the main character from his birth to his death. Defamiliarizing features already surface, however, in the fact that the narrative does not actually begin with the birth of the hero but rather with the sexual act of his conception, thus parodying traditional expositions in this genre. Subsequently, traditional narrative structures and plot patterns are deliberately highlighted and parodied, when Sterne, for example, inserts the preface and the dedication of the novel in the middle of the text and places chapters 18 and 19 after chapter 25. In addition, Sterne introduces *lacunae*, blank spaces, which have to be filled by the reader's imagination, into the text. These elements play with the familiar conventions of the early novel, while simultaneously laying bare the novel's fundamental structures and reminding the reader of the artificiality of the literary text. In modern literary criticism, this self-reflexiveness is often labeled **metafiction** (writing about writing). This term is commonly used to refer to literary works which reflect on their own narrative elements, such as language, narrative structure, and development of plot. In postmodern texts of the second half of the twentieth century, metafictional traits become so common that they almost function as *leitmotifs* (dominant features) of the period.

Russian Formalism's central concept of defamiliarization in many respects anticipates the Brechtian notion of the **alienation effect**, which – leaving its idiosyncrasies aside – also attempts to foreground self-reflexive elements of a text or work of art. Like the proponents of Russian Formalism, the playwright and theoretician Bertold Brecht (1898–1956) is concerned with ways of demonstrating the artificiality of literary discourse. He demanded that, in dramatic performances, actors – and above all the audience – should maintain a critical distance from the play. Brecht carefully positioned alienating elements to remind the spectator of the artificial and illusory nature of a theatrical performance.

Formalism also tries to analyze structurally elements of a text, such as characters in a plot, which older schools traditionally explain on a merely thematic level. Vladimir Propp's (1896–1970) character typology, which reduces the indefinite number of characters in literary works to a limited list of recurrent types, became one of the most influential contributions of Russian Formalism to the general structuralist theories of the twentieth century. This kind of analysis attempts to narrow down the infinite number of possible literary characters to a finite number of basic structural agents including villain, donor, helper, princess, hero and false hero.

The principle of this procedure is based on **Myth Criticism**, which analogously tries to restrict thematic phenomena to formal structures. Similar to Propp's character typology, Myth Criticism exposes patterns of myth – as for example, the mother–son relationship and patricide in the myth of Oedipus – as deep structures underlying a variety of texts. The most famous and influential example of this approach is J.G. Frazer's (1854–1941) voluminous work, *The Golden Bough* (1890–1915), which tries to reveal the common structures of myths in different historical periods and geographical areas. A continuation of Propp's character typology and Frazer's myth analysis was carried out in the 1950s and 1960s by Claude Lévi-Strauss (*1908) in *Structural Anthropology* (1958), which also refers to basic mythological patterns in its description and analysis of cultures. The most influential contribution offered by the mythological approach to literary criticism, however, is the work of Northrop Frye (1912–91), who places structures of myth at the heart of what he considers the main literary genres. According to Frye, the forms of comedy, romance, tragedy and irony (i.e., satire) resemble the patterns of the seasons (spring, summer, autumn and winter, respectively) in primordial myth.

**Archetypal Criticism**, based on C.G. Jung's (1875–1961) deep-psychology, works along similar lines by searching texts for collective motifs of the human psyche, which are held to be common to different historical periods and languages. These archetypes represent primordial images of the human unconscious which have retained their structures in various cultures and epochs. Archetypes such as shadow, fire, snake, paradise-garden, hell, mother-figure, and so on constantly surface in myth and literature as a limited number of basic patterns of psychic images which lend themselves to a structural model of explanation.

In line with this approach, one could, for example, interpret Edgar Allan Poe's (1809–49) short story "The Cask of Amontillado" (1846) with reference to collective archetypes. Poe tells the story of a man who is lured into an subterranean wine cellar by a friend under the pretext of wine tasting; instead, his friend buries him there alive. Having been tricked, he enjoys the wine and foolishly faces death with a laugh. When analyzing these images, it becomes evident that Poe reworked concepts which are deeply rooted in myth and religion: death as a crypt-like underground chamber, wine which dulls the fear of approaching death, and laughter in the face of death. These images surface in the Christian Eucharist, too, which employs a stylized consumption of wine to symbolize resurrection, thus turning the grave into a womb from which the deceased is reborn.

As is evident from this example concerning death and resurrection, various cultures, religions, myths, and literatures have recourse to primordial images or archetypes which – like a subconscious language – express human fears and hopes. The aim of archetypal criticism is in line with the methodology of formalist schools, which delve beneath the surface of literary texts in their search for recurrent deep structures.

### d) New Criticism

Largely independent of European Formalism and Structuralism, the **New Criticism** established itself as the dominant school of literary criticism in the English-speaking academic community during the 1930s and 1940s. Literary critics such as William K. Wimsatt (1907–75), Allen Tate (1899–1979) and J.C. Ransom (1888–1974) represented this school, which maintained its status as an orthodox method for more than three decades. The central features of New Criticism – whose name deliberately negates preceding critical methods – are best understood in contrast to the academic approaches in literary studies which were prevalent in the preceding years. New Criticism objects to evaluative critique, source studies, investigations of socio-historic background, and the history of motifs; it also counters author-centered biographical or psychological approaches as well as the history of reception. Its main concern is to free literary criticism of extrinsic factors and thereby shift the center of attention to the literary text itself.

New Criticism disapproves of what are termed the *affective fallacy* and the *intentional fallacy* in traditional analyses of texts. The term **affective fallacy** stigmatizes interpretive procedures which take into account the emotional reaction of the reader. In this respect, New Criticism does away with the use of ungrounded subjective emotional responses caused by lyrical texts as an analytical "tool." In order to maintain an objective stance, the critic must focus solely on textual idiosyncrasies. The term **intentional fallacy** is applied by interpretive methods which try to recover the original intention or motivation of an author while writing a particular text. New Criticism therefore does not try to match certain aspects of a literary work with biographical data or psychological conditions of the author; instead, its aim is the analysis of a text – seen as a kind of message in a bottle without a sender, date, or address – based solely on the text's intrinsic dimensions.

In its analyses, New Criticism therefore focuses on phenomena such as multiple meaning, paradox, irony, word-play, puns, or rhetorical figures, which – as the smallest distinguishable elements of a literary work – form interdependent links with the overall context. A central term often used synonymously with New Criticism is **close reading**. It denotes the meticulous analysis of these elementary features, which mirror larger structures of a text. New Criticism thus also objects to the common practice of paraphrase in literary studies since this technique does not do justice to such central elements of a work as multiple meaning, paradox, or irony. Another recurrent term in new critical interpretations is **unity**, which originally goes back to Aristotle's *Poetics*. The elements mentioned above underlying *close reading* supposedly reflect the unified structure of the entire literary text.

Poetry in particular lends itself to this kind of interpretation since a number of genre-specific features like rhyme, meter, and rhetorical figures call attention to the closed or unified character of this genre. This is why New Criticism focuses predominantly on poems. Famous examples of new critical analyses are a number of readings of John Keats' (1795–1821) "Ode on a Grecian Urn" (1820). In this poem, Keats describes an ancient vase whose round and self-contained form functions as a symbol for the closed unity of the ideal poem. A new critical interpretation therefore tries to explain the different metrical, rhetorical, stylistic and thematic features as partial aspects of the poem's unity (see also Chapter 2.2: Poetry).

Among the formalist schools, New Criticism is particularly distinguished by the rigidity of its rules for textual analysis. Its applicable methodology and clear guidelines, however, are mainly responsible for the dominant position it held until the late 1960s in English and American universities. It was pushed into the background by reader-oriented approaches as well as by newer text-centered schools. These recent text-oriented trends are often subsumed under the term *post-structuralism* not only because they come *after* the above-mentioned structuralist schools but also because they adapt structuralist methodology for purposes which go *beyond* those originally intended approaches.

### e) Semiotics and Deconstruction

**Semiotics** and **Deconstruction** are the most recent trends in text-oriented literary theory of the 1970s and 1980s, which regards a text as a system of **signs**. The basis for these complex theoretical constructs is the linguistic model of Ferdinand de Saussure (1857–1913). The Swiss linguist starts from the assumption that language functions through representation, in which a mental image is verbally manifested or represented. Before a human being can, for example, use the word "tree" he or she has to envision a mental concept of a tree. Building on this notion, Saussure distinguishes between two fundamental levels of language by referring to the pre-linguistic concept (in this case the mental image of a tree) as the **signified** and its verbal manifestation (the sequence of the letters or sounds T-R-E-E) as the **signifier**.

mental concept or
**signified** (French *signifié*)

linguistic realization or
**signifier** (French *signifiant*)                    T-R-E-E

Saussure introduces a similar dichotomy in his two-leveled structural explanation of language as a means of communication. The conceptual level of *langue* provides the necessary abstract rules and methods of combination which are eventually realized by *parole* in individual spoken or written utterances.

Semiotics and Deconstruction use the verbal sign or *signifier* as the starting point of their analyses, arguing that nothing exists outside the text, i.e., that our perception of the world is of a textual nature. According to these schools, language or texts function in a way that resembles a game of chess. A limited number of signs, like the figures on a chessboard, only make sense when they are in a closed system. Language and text are viewed as part of a system whose meaning is created by the interaction of its different signs as well as the internally distinct features of its elements. This model of explanation is based on the principle of *binary opposition*. The term refers to the elementary distinctness of linguistic signs which cause difference in meaning. In the minimal pairs "h*u*t" / "h*a*t" or "*p*ull" / "*b*ull," for example, only one letter or sound (phoneme) is responsible for differentiating between the meaning of similar combinations of letters.

A new and unconventional aspect of Semiotics and Deconstruction is their attempt to extend the traditional notion of textuality to non-literary or non-linguistic sign systems. Semiotic methods of analysis which originated in literary criticism have been applied in anthropology, the study of popular culture (e.g., advertisements), geography, architecture, film, and art history. The majority of these approaches emphasize the systemic character of the object under analysis. Buildings, myths, or pictures are regarded as systems of signs in which elements interact in ways analogous to letters, words, and sentences. For this reason, these divergent disciplines are often subsumed under the umbrella-term **Semiotics** (the science of signs).

A practical example of the analysis of non-linguistic sign systems is Roland Barthes' (1915–80) semiotics of fashion. This French literary critic regards clothes or garments as systems of signs whose elements can be "read" just like the literary signs of texts. A few millimeters' width of a tie contains complex information. For example, a narrow leather tie conveys a completely different message than a short, wide tie, or a bow-tie does. These textile signs – just like words of a language – can only transmit meaning when seen in their particular context or sign system. Signs therefore only generate meaning when interacting with other signs. Fashion, as a manifestation of social relations, provides a good example for these mechanisms in a non-linguistic system. The signs as such remain the same over the years, but their meaning varies when the relationships between them change. Thus, wide pants, short skirts, or narrow ties convey messages which differ from those they conveyed a few years earlier.

Like Semiotics, **Deconstruction** also highlights the building-block character of texts whose elements consist of signs. This poststructuralist method of analysis starts with the assumption that a text can be analyzed (destructed) and put together (constructed). According to Deconstruction, the text does not remain the same after its reconstruction, since the analysis of signs and their re-organization in the interpretative process is like a continuation of the text itself. Traditional divisions into primary and secondary literature therefore dissolve when one regards interpretation as a continuation or integral part of the text.

Deconstruction is intricately interwoven with the works of the French philosopher Jacques Derrida (*1930) and the literary theorist Paul de Man (1919–83). This approach does not provide any clear-cut guidelines for the analysis of texts and does not consider itself to be a monolithic method or school. Despite the complexity of its philosophical bases, Deconstruction developed into one of the most influential theoretical trends in literary criticism during the 1970s and 1980s and has continued to provide basic notions and terminology for recent publications on literature.

An important example is Derrida's concept of **différance**. While Saussure saw a *signified* (mental concept) behind every *signifier* (sign) in order to explain meaning, Deconstruction deliberately does away with the signified by privileging the interaction between signifiers. Sometimes the concept of an encyclopedia is used to explain how meaning is derived in this system of interdependent signs. Every entry or signifier is embedded in a network of cross-references, each of which in turn contains a number of further references. The meaning of a specific term, therefore, evolves in the continuous process of referring to other terms or signifiers. The neologism *différance* conflates the words "to defer" and "to differ," thereby pointing out both the constant "deferral" to other signifiers and the "difference" that necessarily distinguishes the various signifiers in the system from each other. According to this model of explanation, meaning is generated through reference and difference.

Playful adaptations of this theory are the "dictionary novels" such as *The Dictionary of the Chasars* (1984) by the Serb author Milorad Pavic (*1929) or Walter Abish's (*1931) *Alphabetical Africa* (1974). These texts adopt the external form and structure of a dictionary or encyclopedia in order to highlight the postmodern theoretical notions of text in their own literary medium. Dictionary novels can be read either from beginning to end in a linear way, or by starting somewhere in the middle of the text and moving back and forth from cross-reference to cross-reference.

This cluster of text-oriented theories emphasizes intrinsic dimensions of literary works. Their main objective lies in the analysis of basic textual structures (narrative techniques, plot patterns, point of view, style, rhetorical figures) as well as in the differences between everyday and literary language or between prose and poetry. Semiotics and Deconstruction represent the most extreme examples of text-oriented literary criticism, which, by extending the term "text" to non-literary sign systems, provide textual modes of explanation for different cultural phenomena.

## 2 Author-oriented approaches

In the nineteenth century, before the major formalist-structuralist theories of twentieth century, biographical criticism evolved and became a dominant movement. This **author-oriented approach** established a direct link between the literary text and the biography of the author. Dates, facts and events in an author's life are juxtaposed with literary elements of his or her works in order to find aspects which connect the biography of the author with the text. Research into the milieu and education of the author is conducted and then related to certain phenomena in the text. In addition, an author's library can be examined in order to gain insight into the author's background reading or letters and diaries may be consulted for personal reflections.

Autobiographies are obviously suitable for this kind of approach, which compares the fictional portrayal with the facts and figures from the author's life. In many cases, autobiographical material enters the fictional text in codes. The American playwright Eugene O'Neill (1888–1953), for example, used veiled autobiographical elements in his play *Long Day's Journey into Night* (*c.* 1941; published 1956). Although the characters and events in the play are supposedly fictional, they are based on real people and dramatize events from his family life.

Author-centered approaches focus also on aspects which might have entered the text on a subconscious or involuntary level. The fact that Mary Shelley (1797–1851) had a miscarriage during the period in which she wrote her novel *Frankenstein* (1818) can be related directly to the plot. According to the author-centered approaches, the central theme of the novel, the creation of an artificial human being, can be traced back to Mary Shelley's intense psychological occupation with the issue of birth at the time. Many authors wish to keep their texts fictional and their private spheres intact and hence oppose these approaches. For example, the American author J.D. Salinger (*1919), who became famous with the publication of his novel *The Catcher in the Rye* (1951), has strictly refused to make public any information about his private life over the last decades.

Canonical authors in particular – those who are highly regarded in literary criticism, like Shakespeare, Milton or Joyce – often tend to be mythologized. This leads to attempts to reconstruct the author's spirit through his work. **Phenomenological approaches** assume that the author is present in his text in encoded form and that his spirit can be revived by an intensive reading of his complete works.

As the example from Mary Shelley's life shows, many biographical approaches also tend to employ psychological explanations. This has led to **Psychoanalytic Literary Criticism**, a movement which sometimes deals with the author, but primarily attempts to illuminate general psychological aspects in a text that do not necessarily relate to the author exclusively. Under the influence of Sigmund Freud (1856–1939), Psychoanalytic Literary Criticism expanded the study of psychological features beyond the author to cover a variety of intrinsic textual aspects. For instance, characters in a text can be analyzed psychologically, as if they were real people. An example which has often been cited in this context is the mental state of Hamlet in Shakespeare's (1564–1616) drama; psychoanalytic critics ask whether Hamlet is mad and, if so, from which psychological illness he is suffering.

Sigmund Freud, too, borrowed from literary texts in his explanation of certain psychological phenomena. Some of his studies, such as the analysis of E.T.A. Hoffmann's (1772–1822) story "The Sandman" (1817), rank among the classical interpretations of literary texts. In the second half of the twentieth century, Psychoanalytic Literary Criticism regained momentum under the influence of the French analyst Jacques Lacan (1901–81), especially in the Anglo-American world. The interest in psychological phenomena indirectly abetted the spread of the so-called reader-centered approaches. Their focus on the reception of a text by a reader or on the reading process can therefore be seen as investigations of psychological phenomena in the widest sense of the term.

## 3 Reader-oriented approaches

As a reaction to the dominant position of text-oriented New Criticism, a **reader-oriented approach** developed in the 1960s called **Reception Theory**, Reader-Response Theory or Aesthetics of Reception. All three terms are used almost synonymously to summarize those approaches which focus on the reader's point of view. Some of these approaches do not postulate a single objective text, but rather assume that there are as many texts as readers. This attitude implies that a new individual "text" evolves with every individual reading process.

With the focus on the effect of a text on the recipient or reader, reception theory is obviously opposed to New Criticism's dogma of *affective fallacy*, which demands an interpretation free of subjective contributions by the reader. Reader-centered approaches examine the readership of a text and investigate why, where and when it is read. They also examine certain reading practices of social, ethnic or national groups. Many of these investigations also deal with and try to explain the physiological aspect of the actual reading process. They aim at revealing certain mechanisms which are employed in the transformation of the visual signs on paper into a coherent, meaningful text in the mind of the reader.

These approaches assume that a text creates certain expectations in the reader in every phase of reading. These expectations are then either fulfilled or left unfulfilled. Wolfgang Iser's (*1926) term of the **blank** refers to this phenomenon of expectation stimulated by the text and "filled" by the reader. This principle of the blank can be applied to the elementary level of the sentence as well as to more complex units of meaning. While reading even the first words of a sentence, the reader continually imagines how it might continue. In every phase, the reader attempts to complement what is missing through his own imagination and skill at combination. Similarly, we continually pick up open questions which are then connected to various explanatory options. The filling of the blanks, on the one hand, depends on subjective-individual traits and, on the other, on more general features, such as education, age, gender, nationality, and the historical period of the reader.

The reader's expectation plays a role in every sort of text, but it is most obvious in literary genres like detective fiction, which depends very much on the interaction between text and recipient. Edgar Allan Poe's (1809–49) "The Murders in the Rue Morgue" (1841), for example, consists of several blanks of this sort which consistently guide the reader's imagination and expectation in different directions. A viciously mutilated body is found in a Paris apartment. The reconstruction of the murder and the discovery of the culprit are founded on a number of contradictory testimonies and circumstantial evidence; the reader is continually forced to change assumptions in order to identify the murderer's motive and identity.

Playing with the reader's expectations occupies the foreground in detective fiction but is also present in any other literary genres, though in varying intensity and clarity. Expectations are at the basis of text interpretation on every level of the reading process, from the deciphering of a single word or sentence to the analysis of thematic structures of texts. Reception Theory, therefore, shifts the focus from the text to the interaction between reader and text. It argues that the interpretation of texts cannot and must not be detached from the reading individual.

A further aspect which is closely connected with this movement is the investigation of the reception of texts by a particular readership. In the **History of Reception** sales figures are examined together with reviews in newspapers and magazines. These analyses can either look at the reception of texts in one particular period (synchronic analysis) or trace changes and developments in the reception of texts in literary history (diachronic analysis).

The reader-centered approaches of *Reception Theory* and the *History of Reception*, particularly influential in the 1970s as reactions to the dogmas of New Criticism, were pushed into the background in the 1980s by text-oriented Semiotics and Deconstruction as well as by a variety of context-centered schools.

## 4 Context-oriented approaches

The term **context-oriented approaches** refers here to a heterogeneous group of schools and methodologies which do not regard literary texts as self-contained, independent works of art but try to place them within a larger context. Depending on the movement, this context can be history, social and political background, literary genre, nationality or gender. The most influential movement to this day is **Literary History**, which divides literary phenomena into periods, describes the text with respect to its historical background, dates texts and examines their mutual influence. This movement is associated with the discipline of history and is guided by historical methodology. The entire notion of literary history has become so familiar to us that it is difficult to distinguish it as an approach at all. This historically informed methodology which organizes literary works in a variety of categories is, of course, as arbitrary and subject to conventions as any other approach.

An important school which places literary works in the context of larger socio-political mechanisms is **Marxist Literary Theory**. On the basis of the writings of Karl Marx (1818–83) and literary theoreticians in his wake, including Georg Lukács (1885–1971) and Antonio Gramsci (1891–1937), texts are analyzed as expressions of economic, sociological and political factors. Conditions of production in certain literary periods and their influence on the literary texts of the time are examined. A Marxist literary interpretation, for example, might see the development of the novel in the eighteenth century as a consequence both of new economic conditions for writers and readers and of new modes in the material production of printed books. The Frankfurt School, whose Marxist theoreticians include Theodor Adorno (1900–69) and Jürgen Habermas (*1929) have exerted a major influence on English and American literary criticism. Independent of the fall of the Eastern block, however, Marxist Literary Theory has lost much of its former impact over the last two decades.

Since the mechanisms of class, on which Marxist theory focuses, often parallel the structural processes at work in "race" and "gender," the theoretical framework provided by Marxist criticism has been adapted by younger schools that focus on marginalized groups, including feminist, African American, gay and lesbian literary criticism or colonial literary studies. Text-oriented theoretical approaches such as Deconstruction and New Historicism are also indebted to Marxist thought, both for their terminology and philosophical foundations.

### a) New Historicism

One of the latest developments in the field of contextual approaches has been **New Historicism**, which arose in the USA in the 1980s. It builds on Poststructuralism and Deconstruction, with their focus on text and discourse, but adds a historical dimension to the discussion of literary texts. Certain works by Shakespeare, for instance, are viewed together with historical documents on the discovery of America, and the discovery itself is treated as a text. History, therefore, is not regarded as isolated from the literary text in the sense of a "historical background" but rather as a textual phenomenon. For example, one of the leading figures in New Historicism, Stephen Greenblatt (*1943), has analyzed a colonial text of early American literature by Thomas Harriot (*c*. 1560–1621), comparing the relationship between Europeans and Indians in this text with the structures of dependence in Shakespeare's (1564–1616) play *The Tempest* (*c*. 1611). As a result, the mechanisms of power are exposed as deeply rooted cultural structures which dominate the historical as well as the literary discourses of the time.

New Historicism takes an approach similar to that of the poststructuralist schools, including non-literary phenomena in the definition of "text" and thus treating historical phenomena as they would literary ones. The movement is comparatively new and, like deconstruction, opposed to rigid methods associated with a particular school.

Related to New Historicism, although an independent movement, are **Cultural Studies**, which have advanced to one of the most influential areas within literary studies, if not the humanities as such, in the 1990s. Although firmly rooted in literary studies this approach deliberately analyzes the different aspects of human self-expression, including the visual arts, film, TV, commercials, fashion, architecture, music, popular culture, etc. as manifestations of a cultural whole. In contrast to Semiotics, which is equally interested in non-literary phenomena from a text-oriented, structuralist approach, Cultural Studies adopts a comprehensive perspective, which attempts to grasp culture's multi-faceted nature. As early as 1958 the theorist Raymond Williams (1921–88) in *Culture and Society* argued in favor of a cultural understanding which takes into consideration the whole of cultural production rather than isolated details. This evidently context-oriented approach considers literature as an important, but not the only manifestation of larger cultural mechanisms. In recent years Cultural Studies in literature has been closely connected with the Indian theorist Homi Bhabha (*1949), who incorporates ideas of Poststructuralism and Deconstruction for his theory of culture and cultural identity. His notion of culture as a phenomenon determined by discursive forces shows striking structural analogies to trends in recent gender studies.

## b) Feminist Literary Theory and Gender Theory

The most productive and, at the same time, most revolutionary move-ment of the younger theories of literary criticism in general and the contextual approaches in particular is **Feminist Literary Theory**. This complex critical approach is part of a movement which has established itself in almost all academic disciplines and has become particularly strong in the various branches of modern literary criticism.

Although gender is always at the center of attention in this school, this particular movement may be used to demonstrate how different approaches in literary studies tend to overlap. Feminist Literary Theory starts with the assumption that "gender difference" is an aspect which has been neglected in traditional literary criticism and, therefore, argues that traditional domains of literary criticism have to be re-examined from a gender-oriented perspective.

At the beginning of this movement in the late 1960s, thematic issues such as the portrayal of women in literary texts by male authors stood in the foreground. These early attempts of feminist literary criticism concentrated on stereotypes or distorted portrayals of women in a literary tradition dominated by men. One of the main issues of this reader-centered attitude is the identification of the woman reader with fictional female characters in literary texts.

The next phase in Feminist Literary Theory, the use of histor-ical and author-centered approaches, can be described as *Feminist Literary History* and canon revision, whose primary goal was to estab-lish a new set of standard texts by non-male authors. Feminist literary critics in the mid-1970s drew attention to neglected female authors in the English tradition and propagated a new literary history by focusing on an independent female literary tradition. This kind of feminist literary criticism with a focus on the revision of the canon remained the dominant movement up to the late 1970s, when it was weakened and diverted under the influence of French feminists.

With the American reception of French feminists such as Hélène Cixous (*1937) and Julia Kristeva (*1941), who have strong back-grounds in psychoanalysis and philosophy, the focus of feminist literary criticism shifted at the beginning of the 1980s to textual-stylistic reflections. Assuming that gender difference determines the act of writing, i.e., the style, narrative structure, contents and plot of a text, feminist literary criticism entered domains which are usually treated by text-oriented formalist-structuralist schools. This movement in feminism views the female physical anatomy as responsible for a specifically feminine kind of writing that manifests itself in plot, contents, narrative structure and textual logic. This theoretical assumption is commonly referred to by its French term *ècriture fèminine* ("female writing").

Later works of this movement, which endeavor to account for the position of men in literary criticism and in feminism, produced one of the most distinctive paradigm changes in this field by shifting the emphasis from Feminist Theory to Gender Theory. In **Gender Theory** the object of analysis is no longer the female alone, but rather the interaction of the two genders. An increasing number of male critics are now working on gender problems, thus integrating masculinity into gender studies. In accord with these latest developments, the role of male and female homosexuality in literature and literary criticism receives a great deal of attention.

The most recent trends in Gender Theory incorporate concepts of deconstruction, thus questioning the entire notion of a stable gender identity. This discussion which was initiated by the American literary theorist Judith Butler (*1956) approaches gender identity in a manner reminiscent of deconstruction explaining meaning in language. Gender is thus "constructed" through a number of interacting elements within a societal system. The key term is "gender construction" according to which "man" and "woman" adopt the role of signifiers whose meaning or identity is construed through an interdependent network of other signifiers.

In summary, one can point out a few tendencies which have developed in feminist literary theory since the end of the 1960s: the first cluster of publications in the field focused primarily on what is specifically female (protagonist, author, canon), followed by the poetic-aesthetic theories based on gender-difference (*ècriture fèminine*). As far as we can see today, the latest development is toward a comprehensive view of the importance of both "genders" in the literary production and reception. Although gender studies will always reflect its origins in feminism, recent dialogic trends indicate a shift toward a joint inquiry carried out by scholars of both genders. As feminist literary criticism shows, the distinction between textual, author-centered, reader-centered or contextual approaches cannot always be strictly maintained. In practice, any movement in literary criticism makes use of a combination of a variety of approaches, although one aspect usually dominates and is therefore used to classify the work with a particular school.

So far, the discussion has categorized the various approaches of the different schools according to their common methodological features. What follows is an attempt to list the various movements in the order of their historical succession. The dates given must not be taken as absolute figures; rather, they stand for the periods when the respective movements were at a peak. The majority of the movements mentioned existed simultaneously, with certain schools repeatedly reaching and relinquishing a position of dominance. The historical sequence of the various literary movements shows that there is a constant shifting of focuses and an alteration between text-, author-, reader- and context-oriented approaches. Especially over the last couple of decades, the various movements have changed quickly and have been short-lived, akin to fashions:

| | |
|---|---|
| Antiquity and Middle Ages | Rhetoric |
| Modern times | Philology |
| Nineteenth century | Stylistics |
| | Biographic Criticism |
| First half of twentieth century | Psychoanalytic Criticism |
| | Mythological Criticism |
| c. 1920–30 | Russian Formalism |
| c. 1940–60 | New Criticism |
| c. 1970–80 | Reception Theory |
| c. 1970– | Semiotics |
| | Feminist Literary Theory and Gender Theory |
| | Deconstruction |
| c. 1980– | New Historicism and Cultural Studies |

In the interpretation of literary texts, it is important to decide which approaches are suitable for the text at hand and can lead to new results. Although a text might imply a certain approach because of its thematic, historical or structural qualities, different approaches might often produce more original and rewarding results. Postmodern works ask for a structural approach as they like to play with formal elements. Politically or ideologically motivated texts are ideal for a Marxist approach. Biographies or autobiographies lend themselves to a comparison with the life of the author. In addition, it would seem impossible today to interpret a text by a female author without referring to gender. However, these obvious approaches do not have to dominate the discussion of a text. On the contrary, the choice of methodological approach should be guided primarily by the originality of the results it might produce, while reflecting one's personal interests, the state of current research or the trends of the time.

## 5 Literary critique or evaluation

In the English-speaking world, the term **literary criticism** can refer to the literary interpretation of texts as well as their evaluation. For that reason, **literary critique** is sometimes used to differentiate between the interpretation of a text and the evaluative criticism that often occurs in connection with literary awards and book reviews.

In all philologies (disciplines concerned with the literatures of different countries or ethnic groups) there are publications in weekend editions of major newspapers which introduce the latest in primary or secondary literature in the form of **book reviews**. Among the most distinguished papers in the English-speaking world which review both primary and secondary texts are *The New York Times Book Review* (since 1896), *The New York Review of Books* (since 1963) and *The Times Literary Supplement* (since 1902). Scholarly (secondary) literature is most often reviewed in special journals by literary critics who comment on new book publications in respective fields of research.

Related to book reviews are **review articles**, which discuss a broader theme (such as "Latest Publications in Feminist Literary Theory in English" or "The Phenomenon of New Historicism") or a number of secondary sources on a particular text or author. This kind of general survey offers a basic impression of the latest trends or publications in a certain field.

A similar text type is the reader's review in a publishing house, which is not meant for a general public. Manuscripts which have been submitted to a publisher are evaluated by readers. The tone and style of these evaluations are those of reviews. The following extract from a parodic text by the Italian literary critic and author Umberto Eco (*1932) points out the relativity and limitations of this kind of discourse. It also shows how certain literary methods and approaches are used not just for analysis and interpretation, but also for evaluation and critique. In his "Regretfully, We are Returning . . . Reader's Reports" (1972), Eco wrote a series of fictitious negative reviews of texts belonging to the classical canon of literary history. Eco tries to insinuate what would happen if the classics were submitted to publishers today and rated with conventional methods. He particularly wants to illustrate the relativity of these evaluations by writing, for instance, a fictitious review of the Bible:

> I must say that the first hundred pages of this manuscript really hooked me. Action-packed, they have everything today's reader wants in a good story. Sex (lots of it, including adultery, sodomy, incest), also murder, war, massacres, and so on . . .
>
> But as I kept on reading, I realized that this is actually an anthology, involving several writers, with many – too many – stretches of poetry, and passages that are downright mawkish and boring, and jeremiads that make no sense.
>
> The end is a monster omnibus. It seems to have something for everybody, but ends up appealing to nobody. And acquiring the rights from all these different authors will mean big headaches, unless the editor takes care of that himself. The editor's name, by the way, doesn't appear anywhere on the manuscript, not even in the table of contents. Is there some reason for keeping his identity a secret?
>
> I'd suggest trying to get the rights only to the first five chapters. We're on sure ground there. Also come up with a better title. How about *The Red Sea Desperadoes?* [18]

Here, Eco parodies a reader-centered approach as he investigates the effect of the text on a potential bestseller-public with a strong desire for "sex and crime." The dominating reader-centered approach is, however, interrupted by biographical questions about the authorship of the text and by textual considerations pertinent to stylistic criticism.

Similarly dubious criteria are applied in literary awards. The question concerning the evaluation of texts is as old as literature itself. As early as classical Antiquity, drama contests took place on set occasions to find the best playwright. A classical parody of "objective" criteria of evaluation is Aristophanes' (c. 448–380 BC) comedy *The Frogs* (c. 405 BC), in which Aeschylos and Euripides, the main representatives of Greek drama, engage in a contest. After a series of unsuccessful attempts at finding a winner, the god Dionysus, who is in charge of the contest, chooses an "empirical" method of evaluation: he uses scales to measure the "weight" of the verses. Aeschylos wins the contest because he mentions a river in his verse while Euripides only mentions a boat.

These parodies of literary critique show that the evaluation of texts in literary criticism is controversial, mostly because this process depends on too many variables. Some experimental texts receive bad reviews at the time of their publication, yet prove to be highly valued and influential later on. Book reviews and bestseller lists are relatively short-lived; their importance lies primarily in the information they provide about the reception of a certain text in a specific historical period.

# Chapter 5

# Where and how to find secondary literature

The scholarly analysis of literary works should, ideally, open a new perspective, cast light on a hitherto neglected aspect of a text and establish a connection with the state of current research in the field. In order to meet these requirements, it is necessary to consult the existing secondary literature for results on a certain topic, text or author. The works of previous researchers in a field influence your own work by providing insights related to your topic and thus possibly supporting your particular arguments or by delineating the boundaries of your topic. In some cases a certain topic may have been sufficiently dealt with or treated in much the same way as you had in mind. In such instances, it is necessary to rethink the entire approach or, in the worst case, abandon the project entirely.

Most of these rules for scholarly papers do not apply, of course, in this rigid form to students' writing on a beginner's level. The goal of most lower level seminar papers is to train the student in the techniques and the ethics of scholarly research as well the communication of ideas in writing. Instructors are usually aware that students are in the early stages of learning a difficult craft and therefore do not expect them to be familiar with every piece of secondary material or to make a major contribution to current scholarship in the field. They normally want students of literature to be able to find material on specific topics and apply it according to the general rules of the "craft."

To find secondary literature used in research for most lower level seminars, it is generally sufficient to consult the subject index of the departmental or university library catalogue for the monographic (i.e., book-length) secondary literature on a certain topic. For more elaborate projects – such as master's theses, dissertations and essays to be published in scholarly journals – it is necessary to compile as complete a list of secondary literature as possible. In these advanced research projects, it is important to incorporate the results of other researchers and to ensure that one's own findings are original and hitherto unpublished.

Each philology has bibliographical reference books which can be used to search for further literature. For the study of all modern languages, such as German and Romance languages, and especially for Literatures in English, the *MLA International Bibliography*, compiled by the *Modern Language Association (MLA)*, is the standard work of reference. It has been on the market since 1921 and includes several thousand new entries of secondary literature published every year. Its *Subject Index* permits one to search for secondary literature on a variety of topics, including subjects such as "feminist literary criticism," "detective fiction" or "utopias." The *Author Index* is divided into national literatures and periods, listing the secondary literature which has been published on individual literary texts in the course of a certain year.

For example, in order to find out what was published in 1989 on the novel *The Handmaid's Tale* (1985) by the Canadian author Margaret Atwood (*1939), it is necessary to search under the section "Canadian Literature" in the *Author Index*. This section is further divided into periods. Atwood is a contemporary author and appears, therefore, in the section "1900–1999." Under her name, you find a list of the secondary literature on her respective literary works. For

1989, the *MLA International Bibliography* provides eight entries on Margaret Atwood's *The Handmaid's Tale*. All entries in this standard work are structured like the following sample:

> **Ketterer, David. "Margaret Atwood's *The Handmaid's Tale*: A Contextual Dystopia." *SFS*. 1989 July; 16 (2 [48]): 209–217. [†Dystopian novel. Treatment of historicity.]**

The individual references of the *MLA Bibliography* contain rudimentary information about the contents and topic of the secondary text; most importantly, however, they provide the necessary dates and references for the successful retrieval of secondary literature (which can either be essays or book-length studies). In the example above, the name of the essay's author (Ketterer, David) is mentioned first, then the title of the essay ("Margaret Atwood's *The Handmaid's Tale:* A Contextual Dystopia") followed by the name of the journal or anthology where the essay was published *(SFS* is the abbreviation for *Science-Fiction Studies)*. Finally, the year, volume and pages of the journal are mentioned (1989 July; 16(2[48]): 209–217). For book publications, the place of publication and the publisher are listed too. Finally, the entry provides brief information concerning the contents and topic of the secondary text [†Dystopian novel. Treatment of historicity]. These keywords offer a first quick insight into the relevance of a secondary text for one's own personal research.

If a complete list of secondary literature about an author or text is required, it is necessary to consult all annual volumes by repeating the process described above. As the *MLA International Bibliography* dates back to the year 1921, this can become very time-consuming. In our example, it is sufficient to check the volumes from 1985 onwards, as Atwood's *The Handmaid's Tale* was published in this year and hence no prior entries appear.

Most university and departmental libraries have the *MLA International Bibliography* in its printed version. It is now also possible to consult this source of reference on a CD-ROM disc or online. This computerized database simplifies the search process and the compiling of bibliographies in an unprecedented way, as it is no longer necessary to check each separate volume. All one has to do is enter the name of the author together with the title of the literary text or a subject keyword in order to retrieve a list of published secondary literature on the required item.

Here the above example is given as an entry in the CD-ROM version of the *MLA-Bibliograhy*. The abbreviations on the left margin stand for: TI=title, AU=author(s), SO=source, IS=International Standard Numbers, LA=language, PT=publication type, PY=publication year, DE=descriptors.

> TI: Margaret Atwood's The Handmaid's Tale: A Contextual Dystopia
>
> AU: Ketterer,-David
>
> SO: Science-Fiction-Studies, Greencastle, IN (SFS). 1989 July, 16:2 (48), 209–217
>
> IS: 0091–7729
>
> LA: English
>
> PT: journal-article
>
> PY: 1989
>
> DE: Canadian-literature; 1900–1999; Atwood,-Margaret; The Handmaid's-Tale; novel-; dystopian-novel; treatment of historicity

Most libraries have a CD-ROM version of the *MLA International Bibliography* covering the period from 1963 onwards. If it is necessary to include secondary literature published prior to that year, one must resort to the printed version for the time span not included in this new computerized system. One may also perform an online search of other databases. Many university libraries offer facilities which grant the researcher additional access to extensive international computerized databases and bibliographies. This complex search method is of little interest for the beginner and is probably only worthwhile in the context of a larger research project, such as a thesis or dissertation.

Although the *MLA International Bibliography* is the most comprehensive reference work for modern languages and literatures and usually suffices for the needs of the beginner, it does not, of course, list *all* published items of secondary literature. An easy and fast way to find book-length publications on a specific topic is using online searches on the internet, which combines a number of large research library catalogues (e.g. *Library of Congress, British Library* etc.). Most university libraries provide links to *Online Public Access Catalogue (OPAC)* or *Online Computer Library Center (OCLC)*. These networks allow you to screen different library catalogues simultaneously by simply filing one search. The program then systematically checks the different library holdings for the requested key words. These online searches are particularly helpful when looking for book-length studies published before the 1960s and therefore not listed in the CD-ROM or online versions of the *MLA Bibliography*.

For larger research projects that require complete – or nearly so – lists of secondary literature, it is necessary to consult other printed or computerized general bibliographical sources or specific reference works which specialize in certain areas. The best guide book to these sources is James L. Harner's *Literary Research Guide: An Annotated Listing of Reference Sources in English Literary Studies*, 3rd ed. (New York: MLA, 1998) 900 pp.

Once references to secondary literature have been found in the *MLA Bibliography* (or any other standard reference work), the search for this literature in the departmental or university library begins. If it is necessary to use books or journals which are not available in the home institution, it is possible to order them at the main university library through the "inter-library loan system." This process usually takes considerable time, since books or photocopies of articles have to be ordered from other institutions.

# Chapter 6

# How to write a scholarly paper

To write a successful seminar paper or scholarly essay in the field of literature, one should observe a few conventions. Most importantly, the paper has to be logically structured and easy for the reader to follow. To make the logic of the paper's structure immediately obvious for the reader, the first or **introductory paragraph** should provide a "map" or preview of the structure and content of your paper. One part of the introductory paragraph, the **topic statement**, informs the reader about the subject matter of the paper. Here it is crucial to choose a practicable and sensible focus for your research project. Effective scholarly papers impress through a clear-cut focus on a particular issue. For example, there is little use in choosing a topic as undifferentiated as "Eugene O'Neill's Drama *The Emperor Jones*" for a seminar paper. Taking into consideration the numerous publications on this particular drama, it is essential to concentrate on one particular aspect for analyzing the text, as for example, "C.G. Jung's Archetypes and Eugene O'Neill's *The Emperor*

*Jones*." Of course, you should not select the focus of the paper indiscriminately. On the contrary, ideally the paper should tackle a new as well as central aspect of the text.

An additional part of the introductory paragraph is the **thesis statement** in which you explain how you approach your topic, i.e. which method you use in your analysis and what aspects you present in what sequence. In the introductory paragraph you therefore not only state the topic but also your methodological choice and the structure of your paper. For the above mentioned essay on O'Neill you could argue in the thesis statement that you will first present biographical facts which document O'Neill's familiarity with the theories of C.G. Jung and then summarize some of Jung's major theoretical positions as a basis for your analysis of the drama *The Emperor Jones*. In the thesis statement, you thus summarize the way in which you are going to present that topic.

The first paragraph should, therefore, address the following questions: "What" is the paper all about? "How," i.e., with what method do you approach the topic? And "when" in the course of the paper are you dealing with which issues? If you answer these questions in your introduction, you will provide a *topic statement*, which immediately informs the reader about the choice of your subject matter, and a *thesis statement*, which outlines your methodological approach as well as sequence of presentation.

Here is a possible introductory paragraph:

| | |
|---|---|
| C.G. Jung's Archetypes and Eugene O'Neill's <u>The Emperor Jones</u> | — title of the paper |
| Since its first appearance more than seventy years ago, Eugene O'Neill's ground-breaking play <u>The Emperor Jones</u> (1920) has been subject to a variety of <u>en vogue</u> critical approaches, many of which today seem outdated or appear as mere fads of critical fashion. However, a reading of this seminal play of the America literary canon parallel to | — transition to the topic statement |

C.G. Jung's concept of archetypes is not only — topic
suggested by the play's content but also by    statement
biographical documents which corroborate
O'Neill's familiarity with and interest in Jung's
theories. I will therefore briefly summarize
O'Neill's contact with Jungian concepts by — thesis
relying on published statements by the author   statement
himself, then sketch some of the major
features of C.G. Jung's notion of the archetype
in order to read select passages of The
Emperor Jones within this theoretical framework.

Every subsequent **paragraph** or section should be a self-contained argument that develops one particular aspect of the overall topic. When you compose a paragraph, check if it is relevant to your topic and if it addresses one of the issues that you raised in the thesis statement. Even on the paragraph level, it is important to guide the reader as much as possible. **Transitions** from one paragraph to the next help to ensure the required inner coherence of the paper and convey a certain security for the reader when advancing through your arguments. Ideally, transitional phrases at the end of each paragraph should establish a connection with the following one, and others at the beginnings of the paragraphs should somehow point back to the previous one. This technique is one of the cornerstones of lucid writing in general; it is not as easy to apply as it sounds, but requires a great deal of practice, patience and persistence.

The first and most obvious visual signs of badly organized writing are single-sentence paragraphs. Try to avoid them by organizing scattered sentences into units of thought. As a kind of checklist for a successful paragraph, you can ask yourself the following questions:

1 Does the paragraph develop a single, coherent aspect of the overall topic or argument?
2 Is the paragraph placed at the correct point in the paper?
3 Does the paragraph begin and end with smooth and logical transitions?

At the end of the essay, a **concluding paragraph** should summarize the most important results of your discussion of the topic. Do not be afraid to tell the reader once again what the main points of your argument were. The reader likes to be reminded of the central issues of your essay to make sure that the main points have been grasped correctly and to help remember them.

Here is a possible concluding paragraph:

| | |
|---|---|
| Obviously, an archetypal reading of Eugene O'Neill's The Emperor Jones cannot account for all of the play's intricacies. However, by juxtaposing biographical | — transition to the conclusion |
| documents of the author in which he expresses a deep interest in Jungian thought, together with a contextual analysis of the forest scenes in the second part of the play, it was possible to trace a striking coincidence between O'Neill's literary images and Jungian theoretical concepts. These images turned out to be | — repetition of the topic and thesis statement |
| deeply rooted in O'Neill's dramatic understanding and thus shed light on some of the governing principles at work in O'Neill's early plays. | — summary of results |

The best way to check if your introduction and conclusion are efficient is to read only the first and last paragraphs of your paper. If these two passages mention all central questions and methodological steps as well as provide a summary of the major results, then introduction and conclusion fulfill their functions; i.e., these two sections of your paper should put into a nutshell the information about content, methodology and results.

You might rightly add that not all published scholarly articles observe this rather rigid structure. However, this composition technique is required in most college courses in England and America.

For the beginner this technique has the advantage that it provides clear-cut rules for enhancing the effectiveness and readability of texts by stressing unity and logic. Although these rules appear simple in theory, they are difficult to put into practice. It is therefore essential not to give up and to keep on trying. This composition technique might appear rather rigid and uncreative at times, but it definitely adds to the coherence and clarity of any kind of scholarly writing, from seminar papers to published essays.

Every academic discipline follows certain conventions in addition to those governing the structure and content of written scholarly discourse, particularly concerning the **documentation of sources**. This feature of scholarly writing is often subsumed under the term **critical apparatus**. In the field of English and American literature, there are particularly strict rules of documentation, which have been published in a handbook by the aforementioned *Modern Language Association*, the largest and most influential association of literary scholars. The *MLA style sheet* serves as the guideline for all major presses and journals publishing on English literature and is followed and taught in most literature departments. The following guidelines are simplified versions of the most important rules that are explained in great detail in the *MLA Handbook for Writers of Research Papers* (1999) (which is separate from the *MLA Bibliography*).[19]

A consistent and accurate *critical apparatus* is, like spelling, one of the few objective criteria in scholarly writing and should therefore be executed very diligently. Although this meticulous emphasis on technicalities might appear of minor importance to the beginner, it is a major issue when it comes to the evaluation of papers by instructors or readers. The critical apparatus must contain all primary and secondary texts used, so as to enable the reader to retrace the sources of quotations and paraphrases at any time. Therefore, it is vital to collect all necessary information concerning a text, such as the author's or editor's name, the title of the text, the journal or anthology containing the essay, the year of publication, the volume and the page numbers. For books, the place of publication and the name of the publisher must to be mentioned, too. This information usually appears in the first pages of a book or in the masthead of a journal.

The literature used in a paper can be incorporated either in the form of direct **quotations** or as **paraphrases**: short passages from primary texts are usually integrated as direct quotations, larger units of meaning as paraphrases. Secondary literature is generally paraphrased, except for important statements which either support or contradict your argument and are therefore sometimes quoted word for word. Try to avoid stringing together too many direct quotes from other people's essays.

In our discussion of the differences between primary and secondary literature, we have already mentioned that the critical apparatus contains footnotes and a bibliography. **Footnotes** (positioned at the bottom of the page), or **endnotes** (positioned at the end of the entire paper), serve a dual function in a scholarly paper: first, they allow you to reveal the source of information or quotations and to refer to further sources; second, they permit you to expand on a thought which is not directly relevant to the general argument in the text. The **bibliography** at the end of a text is an alphabetically arranged documentation of the primary and secondary literature used in the paper.

When documenting sources in footnotes or bibliography, it is necessary to provide all the information in the correct sequence of "who," "what," "where," "when" (author, title, place of publication, name of publisher, and year of publication). Footnotes differ structurally from bibliographical entries in the sequence of first and last names and the use of parentheses and punctuation, as can be seen in the following examples:

*Entry in a* **bibliography**:

Last Name, First Name. Title of the Text. Place of Publication: Name of Publisher, Year of Publication.

Frye, Northrop. <u>Anatomy of Criticism: Four Essays</u>. Princeton: Princeton University Press, 1957.

Because of the alphabetical order of the entries in the bibliography, the last name of the author comes before the first name.

*Example of a* **footnote**:

First Name, Last name, <u>Title of the Text</u> (Place of Publication: Name of Publisher, Year of Publication) Page Number.

[1]Northrop Frye, <u>Anatomy of Criticism: Four Essays</u> (Princeton: Princeton University Press, 1957) 52.

In *footnotes*, the author's first name is mentioned first and the place of publication, the name of the publisher and year of publication appear in parentheses. The positioning of periods and commas also differs from entries in bibliographies. In both notes and bibliographies, titles of book publications and names of journals are always underlined (or italicized in printed papers). Titles of essays appear in standard typeface (without underlining or italics) and are put in quotation marks to distinguish them from book publications. Names of journals are underlined or italicized and are often abbreviated. The *MLA International Bibliography* devotes a complete section to standard abbreviations of all current journals of literary criticism and linguistics.

*Further examples of* **footnotes**:

Book publication by one author:
[1]Carol Fairbanks, <u>Prairie Women: Images in American and Canadian Fiction</u> (New Haven: Yale University Press, 1986) 32.

In order to distinguish a book publication from an essay, the title of a book is underlined.

Anthology by several editors:
[2]LeRoi Jones and Larry Neal, eds., <u>Black Fire: An Anthology of Afro-American Writing</u> (New York: Morrow, 1968) 85.

The abbreviation "eds." after the name stands for the "editors" who have compiled the essays or texts of the anthology.

Essay by two authors in a journal:

[3]W. K. Wimsatt, Jr., and Monroe C. Beardsley, "The Concept of Meter: An Exercise in Abstraction," <u>PMLA</u>, 74 (1959): 593.

The titles of essays are put in quotation marks in order to distinguish them from book publications. The underlined abbreviation <u>PMLA</u> stands for the literary journal *Publications of the Modern Language Association*. "74" is the annual volume, "1959" the year of publication and "593" the page reference.

*Further examples for entries in a* **bibliography**:

Book publication by two authors:

Gilbert, Sandra M., and Susan Gubar. <u>The Madwoman in the Attic: The Woman Writer and the Nineteenth-Century Imagination</u>. New Haven: Yale University Press, 1979.

If the titles of scholarly works consist of two parts, the subtitle is usually separated from the title by a colon (:), as in the preceding example.

Essay in a journal:

Booth, Wayne C. "Kenneth Burke's Way of Knowing." <u>Critical Inquiry</u> 1 (1974): 1—22.

Bibliographical entries have to contain the exact page numbers (from beginning to end) of the quoted essay. In contrast to book publications and anthologies, the name of the publisher and place of publication are never provided for journal articles.

Anthology by one author:

Greenblatt, Stephen, ed. <u>New World Encounters</u>. Berkeley: University of California Press, 1993.

In recent years literary studies, like any other scholarly discipline, have been affected by new electronic media. Some primary and secondary sources are available as online publications or as CD-ROMs. It is therefore essential when citing these new media to follow a consistent format to enable the reader to trace your electronic sources. In general you follow the same pattern as with print publications by citing author, editor, title etc. When referring to CD-ROMs you also have to include "CD-ROM" before mentioning the place of publication:

> CD-ROM as an entry in a bibliopgraphy:
> Braunmuller, A.R., ed. <u>Macbeth</u>. By William Shakespeare. CD–ROM. New York: Voyager, 1994.

Online articles and books are cited as their printed counterparts. However, it is essential to include the date when you accessed the source as well as their *Uniform Resource Locator (URL)*, i.e., its network address. Since online publications can be changed very easily it is important to mention the exact date of access in order to state which version of the document you refer to in your paper:

> Online article as an entry in a bibliography:
> Miles, Adrian. <u>"Singin' in the Rain</u>: A Hypertextual Reading." <u>Postmodern Culture</u> 8.2 (1998). 25 June 1998 <http:// jefferson.village.virginia.edu/pmc/ issue.198/8.2miles.html>.

The examples above cover the most common types of entries in footnotes and bibliographies. Detailed instructions for documenting book reviews, translations, new editions, films, online publications, or compact discs can be found in the *MLA Handbook*. In order to find out how to cite these special cases, it is necessary to consult the detailed alphabetical index at the end of the handbook.

*The MLA Handbook* also offers the option of **parenthetical documentation** instead of foot- or endnotes. This mode of documentation can be used in two ways. If a particular primary or secondary text is mentioned more than once in a scholarly paper, it does not have to be documented as a separate footnote every time, but can be referred to in parenthetical documentation. In this case, either the title of the work and the page reference (<u>Anatomy of Criticism</u>, 22), or the name of the author and the page reference (Frye, 22) are cited directly after the quotation within the text. This format can also be used to abandon footnotes completely, by providing all references to sources in parentheses in the text of the paper. In this case, full documentation of sources is provided only in the bibliography.

Short, direct quotations containing less than four typed lines are generally incorporated in the text and placed in quotation marks. Longer quotations are set off from the text by indenting each line ten spaces from the left margin. If a passage is not quoted as a whole, the omitted parts are indicated by three periods (. . .).

As papers are designed to be corrected or reviewed by readers, double-spaced lines and generous margins on both sides of the text leave room for notes and comments. It is also important to include your name, provide a title for the paper, and indicate the instructor's name as well as the name of the course on the first page or on a separate cover page.

The following are examples of the title page and the bibliography of a seminar paper. The sample title page of a seminar paper on the next page is only meant to illustrate the most common structural features of documentation; it should not be taken as a model for the composition of an introductory paragraph since the spatial restrictions in the layout of the printed page did not permit the inclusion of a full-fledged introductory paragraph with proper thesis and topic statement.

Jones 1 — use consistent
pagination

Chris Jones
Professor Lement
English 210 Contemporary Utopian Fiction
14 Jan. 2000

Gender in Ursula Le Guin's The
Dispossessed

— underline book
titles

Until recently much scholarship of Le
Guin's fiction has tended to touch only on
surface issues, which have taken their bearings
from a critique of the perceived limitations of
her female characters and her inclination
toward an overall "maleness" in her portrayal
of androgynes in The Left Hand of Darkness.

— indent first line
of a paragraph

Although Le Guin took such accusations
seriously – and in her essay "Is Gender
Necessary? Redux," apologized for not having
explored "androgyny from a woman's point of
view as well as a man's"[1] – she also hinted at
the intricate gender pattern in her novel,
when stating that the androgynes

put titles of essays
or short stories in
quotation marks

put short quota-
tions in quotation
marks within the
text

have no myth of progress at all.
Their calendar calls the current year
always the Year One, and they count
backward and forward from that. In this,
it seems that what I was after again
was a balance: the ... linearity of the
"male", the pushing forward to the limit,
... and the circularity of the "female"
("Is Gender Necessary?", 12).

indent longer
quotations
without using
quotation marks

identify omitted
passages with
three periods

use parenthetical
documentation
for frequently
cited texts

1 Ursula K. Le Guin, "Is Gender
Necessary? Redux," Dancing at the Edge of the
World: Thoughts on Words, Women, Places
(New York: Grove, 1989) 7.

Example for a page from a bibliography:

## List of works cited

Bittner, James W. "Chronosophy, Aesthetics, and Ethics in Le Guin's The Dispossessed: An Ambiguous Utopia." No Place Else: Explorations in Utopian and Dystopian Fiction. Ed. Eric S. Rabkin, Martin H. Greenberg and Joseph D. Olander. Carbondale: Southern Illinois University Press, 1983. 244–70.

Derrida, Jacques. Of Grammatology. Trans. Gayatari Chakravorty Spivak. Baltimore: Johns Hopkins University Press, 1974.

Gilman, Charlotte Perkins. Herland. 1915. London: Women's Press, 1986.

Le Guin, Ursula K. The Dispossessed. 1974. London: Grafton, 1986.

—— The Left Hand of Darkness. London: Macdonald, 1969.

—— "Is Gender Necessary? Redux." Dancing at the Edge of the World: Thoughts on Words, Women, Places. New York: Grove, 1989. 7–16.

Moi, Toril. Sexual/Textual Politics. London: Methuen, 1985.

Montrelay, Michèle. "Inquiry into Femininity." French Feminist Thought: A Reader. Ed. Toril Moi. New York: Blackwell, 1987. 227–49.

Showalter, Elaine. "Feminist Criticism in the Wilderness." The New Feminist Criticism. Ed. Elaine Showalter. London: Virago, 1985. 243–70.

Chapter 7

# Suggestions for
# further reading

The works mentioned below are basic study aids and
reference books in English Literature and Film Studies
and can be found in most university and departmental
libraries. The list is, of course, not intended to be
comprehensive. Of the large number of available texts,
only user-friendly works have been selected. Although
general in scope, they nevertheless provide more
focused information on particular topics than the chapters of this introduction.

Works marked with an asterisk are recom-
mended as a first choice for further reading for the
beginner because of their conciseness and clarity.
General reference works precede more focused texts in
the list.

## General literary terminology

*M.H. Abrams, *A Glossary of Literary Terms*, 7th ed. (Fort
Worth, San Diego: Harcourt Brace Jovanovich, 1998);
434 pp.

This comprehensive reference work explains basic literary terminology, introduces the most important theoretical movements in literary criticism and lists titles for further reading; it can be used as a study aid for the beginner and as a terminological reference work throughout one's studies of literature.

J.A. Cuddon, *The Penguin Dictionary of Literary Terms and Literary Theory*, 4th ed. (London, New York: Penguin, 1999); 1024 pp.

This very comprehensive and inexpensive terminological dictionary provides additional information that goes beyond Abrams' survey.

*Encyclopedia of Literature and Criticism*, ed. Martin Coyle *et al.* (London: Routledge, 1993); 1264 pp.

Collection of essays on important issues of literary studies with references for further reading. Besides traditional areas – periods, genres and theories – about 100 pages are devoted to Anglophone literatures outside England and the United States.

## Authors and works

*\*The Oxford Companion to English Literature*, ed. Margaret Drabble, 5th ed. (Oxford, New York: Oxford University Press, 1998); 1216 pp.
*The Oxford Companion to American Literature*, ed. James D. Hart, 6th ed. (Oxford, New York: Oxford University Press, 1995); 880 pp.

These comprehensive, alphabetically arranged reference works provide basic factual information about major English and American authors and literary texts.

*Encyclopedia of Post-Colonial Literatures in English*, eds. Eugen Benson and L.W. Conolly, 2 vols. (London: Routledge, 1994); each volume approx. 900 pp.

An alphabetically arranged reference work on the major regions, authors, themes and genres of literatures in English outside England and the United States. It takes into account recent developments and provides references to secondary sources.

## Literary theory in general

*Critical Theory Since Plato,* ed. Hazard Adams, rev. ed. (Fort Worth, Philadelphia: Harcourt Brace Jovanovich, 1992); 1271 pp.

Collection of theoretical primary texts from classical antiquity to the present time.

*The Johns Hopkins Guide to Literary Theory & Criticism,* eds. Michael Groden and Martin Kreiswirth (Baltimore, London: The Johns Hopkins University Press, 1993); 775 pp.

*Encyclopedia of Contemporary Literary Theory: Approaches, Scholars, and Terms,* ed. Irena R. Makaryk (Toronto, Buffalo, London: University of Toronto Press, 1993); 656 pp.

Comprehensive, alphabetically arranged reference works with short essay-like entries on the most important movements, proponents and terms in literary theory as well as references to further literature.

*Jeremy Hawthorn, *A Concise Glossary of Contemporary Literary Theory,* 3rd ed. (London, New York: Edward Arnold, 1998); 288 pp.

Concise, alphabetically organized survey of the most imporant terms of postmodern literary theory.

*Raman Selden and Peter Widdowson, *A Reader's Guide to Contemporary Literary Theory,* 4th ed. (Lexington: The University Press of Kentucky, 1993); 244 pp.

One of the most lucid introductions to recent literary theory for the beginner. It may be supplemented by:

Raman Selden, *Practicing Theory and Reading Literature: An Introduction* (Lexington: The University Press of Kentucky, 1989); 218 pp.

This introductory text applies different critical approaches to major English texts in order to illustrate the possibilities of various methodologies in sample interpretations.

Terry Eagleton, *Literary Theory: An Introduction,* 2nd. ed. (Minneapolis: University of Minnesota Press, 1996); 288 pp.

Widely used introduction to literary theory which provides a thorough and accessible survey of the field.

## Works on specific areas of literary theory

The following texts are introductions to specific areas of literary theory and are slightly more demanding than the surveys mentioned above.

**Structuralist Theory**: Terence Hawkes, *Structuralism and Semiotics* (Berkeley: University of California Press, 1977); 192 pp.

**Psychoanalytic Literary Theory**: Elisabeth Wright, *Psychoanalytic Criticism: Theory and Practice* (London, New York: Methuen, 1984); 208 pp.

**Marxist Literary Theory**: Terry Eagleton, *Marxism and Literary Criticism* (Berkeley: University of California Press, 1976); 88 pp.

**Deconstruction**: Christopher Norris; *Deconstruction: Theory and Practice* (New York: Routledge Chapman & Hall, 1982); 157 pp.

**Feminist Literary Theory**: Toril Moi, *Sexual, Textual Politics* (London, New York: Methuen, 1985); 206 pp.

**Reception Theory**: Robert C. Holub, *Reception Theory: A Critical Introduction* (London, New York: Methuen, 1985); 189 pp.

**New Historicism**: *The New Historicism Reader*, ed. H. Aram Veeser (New York: Routledge, 1994); 376 S.

**Cultural Studies**: Fred Inglis, *Cultural Studies* (Oxford: Blackwell, 1993); 262 S.

**Post-Colonial Theory**: Peter Childs and Patrick Williams, *An Introduction to Post-Colonial Theory* (London, New York: Prentice Hall, 1997); 240 S.

## Collections of primary literary texts in English

*The Norton Introduction to Literature*, eds. Carl E. Bain *et al.* 7th ed. (New York, London: Norton, 1998); 2165 pp.

A collection of primary texts in English, of different genres and periods, with some additional terminological information as well as guidelines for the interpretation of texts.

*The Norton Anthology of English Literature*, eds. M.H. Abrams, *et al.*, 6th ed. 2 vols. (New York, London: Norton, 1993); each volume approx. 2500 pp. *The Norton Anthology of American Literature*, eds. Nina Baym, *et al.*, 5th ed., 2 vols. (New York, London: Norton, 1999); each volume approx. 2500 pp.

*The Norton Anthology of Literature by Women: The Traditions in English*, eds. Sandra M. Gilbert and Susan Gubar, 2nd ed. (New York, London: Norton, 1996); 2452 pp.

These three collections of primary texts in English provide a representative selection of works from different periods and genres. They are also a good means by which the beginner may judge which literary works are traditionally considered canonical, i.e., important texts in the field.

*New Worlds of Literature: Writings from America's Many Cultures*, eds. Jerome Beaty and J. Paul Hunter, 2nd ed. (New York, London: Norton, 1994); 980pp.

An anthology of literary texts in English from the United States, Canada and the Caribbean which deliberately shifts the emphasis from the "Anglo-Saxon" tradition to authors of different ethnic and cultural backgrounds.

## Fiction

*Jeremy Hawthorn, *Studying the Novel: An Introduction*, 3rd ed. (Oxford: Oxford University Press, 1997); 192 pp.

A very basic introduction to the history and the elements of the novel with references for further reading.

Franz Stanzel, *A Theory of Narrative* (Cambridge: Cambridge University Press, 1984); 308 pp.

A rather complex narratological study that tries to put issues concerning *point of view* into a coherent structuralist model of explanation.

*Columbia History of the British Novel*, eds. John J. Richetti *et al.* (New York: Columbia University Press, 1994); 1064 pp.
*Columbia History of the American Novel*, eds. Emory Elliott (New York: Columbia University Press, 1994); 800 pp.

Collections of essays by literary historians on important novelists.

Ian Watt, *The Rise of the Novel: Studies in Defoe, Richardson and Fielding* (Berkeley: University of California Press, 1957); 319 pp.

Classic study on the origins of the English novel and its socio-cultural background in the eighteenth century.

Michael McKeon, *The Origins of the English Novel, 1600–1740* (Baltimore: The Johns Hopkins University Press, 1988); 544 pp.

Study on the early English novel. In contrast to Watt's book, it argues that the genre evolved before the eighteenth century.

## Poetry

*The Princeton Encyclopedia of Poetry and Poetics*, ed. Alex Preminger *et al.*, rev. ed. (Princeton: Princeton University Press, 1993); 1382 pp.

Standard encyclopedic reference work on the major areas of poetry and literary theory.

*\*The Norton Introduction to Poetry*, ed. J. Paul Hunter, 7th ed. (New York, London: Norton, 1998); 656 pp.

Laurence Perrine and Thomas R. Arp, *Sound and Sense: An Introduction to Poetry*, 9th ed. (Fort Worth, Philadelphia: Harcourt Brace Jovanovich, 1996); 401 pp.

Both are introductions to the elements and terminology of poetry with many examples suitable for beginners.

Cleanth Brooks and Robert Penn Warren, *Understanding Poetry*, 4th ed. (New York: Holt, Rinehart and Winston, 1976); 602 pp.

Classic text on the structuralist analysis of poetry, which, despite its rigid approach, offers a good survey of the terminological and formal aspects of poetry as well as illustrative readings of poems.

*The Columbia History of American Poetry*, ed. Jay Parini and Brett C. Miller (New York: Columbia University Press, 1993); 894 pp.

A collection of essays by literary historians on major American poets.

## Drama

*The Cambridge Guide to Theatre*, ed. Martin Banham, 2nd ed. (Cambridge: Cambridge University Press, 1995); 1247 pp.

Illustrated, alphabetically arranged reference work with brief entries on the major playwrights, plays and dramatic terms.

*Oscar G. Brockett, *The Essential Theater,* 6th ed. (Fort Worth: Harcourt Brace College Publishers, 1996); 495 pp.
Robert Cohen, *Theater: Brief Version,* 4th ed. (Palo Alto: Mayfield Publishing Company, 1996); 348 pp.
Robert W. Corrigan, *The World of Theater,* 2nd ed. (Madison: Brown & Benchmark, 1992); 408 pp.

These three books are richly illustrated, comprehensive introductions to drama. They go beyond the narrow English and American context and also include aspects of directing and performance.

Martin Esslin, *An Anatomy of Drama* (New York: Hill & Wang, 1977); 125 pp.

Very concise and accessible first survey of the most important aspects of drama.

Simon Trussler, *The Cambridge Illustrated History of British Theatre* (Cambridge: Cambridge University Press, 1994); 403 pp.
Phyllis Hartnoll, *A Concise History of Theatre,* rev. ed. (London: Thames and Hudson, 1985); 262 pp.

Both books provide comprehensive and richly illustrated histories of theater in England from its beginnings in the Middle Ages to the 1990s.

## Film

*International Dictionary of Films and Filmmakers,* eds. Nicolet V. Elert *et al.,* 3rd ed., 4 vols. (Detroit, New York: St James Press, 1997); each vol. approx. 1250 pp.

Very comprehensive reference work on the different aspects of international film with individual volumes on films, directors, actors, scriptwriters and producers.

Ephraim Katz, *The Film Encyclopedia,* 3rd ed. (New York: Harper Perennial, 1998); 1506 pp.

Affordable, alphabetically organized reference work on the most important terms, people and works in the film industry and film criticism.

Leonard Martin, *Movie and Video Guide* (New York: Signet, 1999); 1648 pp.
Very inexpensive, annually published (and therefore up-to-date) reference work on the most important movies and video films.

*David Parkinson, *History of Film* (New York: Thames and Hudson, 1995); 264 pp.
Very concise and richly illustrated survey of the history of international film.

Gerald Mast and Bruce F. Kawin, *A Short History of the Movies,* 6th ed. (Boston, London: Allyn & Bacon, 1996); 724 pp.
David A. Cook, *A History of Narrative Film*, 3rd. ed. (New York, London: W.W. Norton, 1996); 1087 pp.
Both comprehensive and accessible surveys of the history of international film.

*Thomas Sobchack and Vivian Sobchack, *An Introduction to Film,* 2nd ed. (Glenview, Boston: Scott, Foresman and Company, 1994); 514 pp.
Luis Giannetti, *Understanding Movies*, 7th ed. (Englewood: Prentice-Hall, 1995); 512 pp.
Bruch F. Kawin, *How Movies Work* (Berkeley, Los Angeles: University of California Press, 1992); 574 pp.
These three books provide lucid introductions to the history, genres and elements of film with many examples and illustrations.

James Monaco, *How to Read a Film: The Art, Technology, Language, History and Theory of Film and Media*, 2nd ed. (New York, Oxford: Oxford University Press, 1981); 533 pp.
A classic introduction to film.

Morris Beja, *Film and Literature: An Introduction* (London: Longman, 1979); 335 pp.
Survey of the relationship between literature and film, including a number of illustrative readings of film versions of literary texts.

*The Encyclopedia of Novels into Film*, eds. John C. Tibbets and James M. Welsh (New York: Facts on File, 1998); 522 pp.

General reference work on film adaptations of novels, including summaries of the novels and their film versions; very helpful are the short bibliographies of secondary sources on each adaptation.

*Film Theory and Criticism: Introductory Readings*, eds. Leo Braudy and Marshall Cohen, 5th ed. (New York, Oxford: Oxford University Press, 1998); 797 pp.

A collection of illustrative "primary texts" on film theory and film criticism from the birth of the medium to the present.

## Literary history

*G.C. Thornley and Gwyneth Roberts, *An Outline of English Literature*, rev. ed. (London, New York: Longman, 1994); 216 pp.
*Peter B. High, *An Outline of American Literature* (London, New York: Longman, 1986); 256 pp.

Both texts offer concise, illustrated surveys of the most important periods, authors and works in British and American literature from their origins until the present. They are characterized by illustrative readings of texts that shed light on larger mechanisms without giving long lists of dates and facts.

Pat Rogers, ed. *The Oxford Illustrated History of English Literature* (Oxford, New York: Oxford University Press, 1992); 490 pp.
Andrew Sanders, *Short Oxford History of English Literature* (Oxford: Oxford University Press, 1994); 678 pp.

Both very appealing, illustrated collections of essays that cover the major periods of English literary history.

*Columbia Literary History of the United States*, ed. Emory Elliott (New York: Columbia University Press, 1988); 1263 pp.

Single volume, quite demanding standard work with essays on American literature from its beginnings to the present.

*The Cambridge History of American Literature*, ed. Sacvan Bercovitch, 8 vols. (Cambridge: Cambridge University Press, 1994–); each volume approx. 900 pp.

New standard work on American literary history with essays by leading scholars in the field. Not all of the planned eight volumes have been published yet. These complex volumes are not suitable for the beginner but rather are useful for students or scholars who need a specialized survey of a particular period.

## Library resources and style sheets

James L. Harner, *Literary Research Guide: An Annotated Listing of Reference Sources in English Literary Studies*, 3rd ed. (New York: MLA, 1998); 900 pp.

Very detailed compilation of the possible sources for bibliographical searches. It provides lists of general bibliographical works which are similar to the *MLA International Bibliography*, but also mentions a number of other reference works on various disciplines and areas of literary study.

*Joseph Gibaldi, *MLA Handbook for Writers of Research Papers*, 5th ed. (New York: MLA, 1999); 320 pp.

Detailed standard style sheet with formal rules on how to document sources in a literary research paper. This handbook is frequently revised; it is important to use the most recent edition.

Chapter 8

# Glossary of literary and cinematographic terms

This survey of the most important terms in literary criticism and film studies can be used either as a concise reference section or as an aid in self-examination. The numbers refer to the pages in the text where the respective terms are dealt with in more detail.

**acoustic dimension of film**, 65–66: most recently acquired feature of → *film*. Not developed until the 1920s, it radically changed the medium because information no longer had to be conveyed merely by means of visual effects such as facial expression, gestures or subtitles, but could also rely on language (→ *dialogue* and → *monologue)*, music or sound effects.

**act**, 48: major structuring principle of → *drama*; it is traditionally subdivided into → *scenes*. → *Elizabethan Theater* adopted this formal structure from classical antiquity, dividing the → *plot* into five acts; in the nineteenth century, the number of acts was reduced to four; in the twentieth century generally to three. Sometimes acts are abandoned altogether in favor of a loose sequence of scenes.

**actor**, 54: agent that stands at the intersection of → *text*, → *transformation* and → *performance* in → *drama* and thereby distinguishes the → *performing arts* from → *literary texts* in the narrow sense of the term. The actor is the mediator of the combined concerns of the author and the director in the performance, the last phase of drama. Traditional actor training distinguishes between the → *internal method* (with a focus on individual qualities of the actor) and the → *external method* (stressing technique).

**affective fallacy**, 86: "wrong belief in subjective effects"; important term of → *New Criticism,* attacking any kind of → *interpretation* that considers the reader's emotional reactions to a → *text* as relevant in the scholarly analysis of text; see also → *intentional fallacy.*

**alliteration**, 41: type of → *rhyme* in which the first consonant is repeated within the same line; see also → *assonance.*

**amphitheater**, 51: see → *Greek Theater.*

**anapest**, 40: → *foot* in which two unstressed syllables are followed by a stressed syllable (˘˘´), as for example in "Ănd thĕ sheén | ŏf theĭr spéars | wăs lĭke stárs | ŏn thĕ seá".

**Archetypal Criticism**, 84: based on the depth psychology of C.G. Jung (1875–1961), this → *text-oriented approach* analyzes → *texts* according to collective motifs or archetypes of the human unconscious which are shared by various periods and languages and appear in myth and → *literature* (e.g., mother figure, shadow, etc.); see also → *myth criticism.*

**article**, 5: one of the shorter forms of → *secondary source* on a specific topic, → *text* or author published in a → *journal* or → *collection of essays.* The term "article" is used synonymously with → *essay,* which, however, also refers to a semi-literary genre in the seventeenth and eighteenth centuries.

**aside**, 47: form of → *monologue* in → *drama.* It is not meant to be heard by the other figures of the play, providing information only for the audience.

**assonance**, 41: type of → *rhyme* in which the first vowel of a word is repeated later in the same line; see also → *alliteration.*

**author-oriented approaches**, 90–92: movements in → *literary criticism* which try to establish a direct connection between a literary → *text* and the biography of the author; see also → *biographical criticism.*

**ballad**, 31: sub-genre of → *narrative poetry.* It is situated between the longer → *epic* poetry and the shorter → *lyric poetry.* It is characterized by well-rounded → *plots* and complex narrative techniques, but it is not sufficient in range and size to match the proportions of the epic or the →*romance.* It traditionally uses a → *quatrain* form.

**bibliography**, 6, 114–120: or **list of works cited**. Alphabetical list of → *primary* and → *secondary sources* used in a scholarly papers to document sources; see also → *footnotes.*

**Bildungsroman**, 12: German for "novel of education"; the term is also applied in English for a sub-genre of the → *novel* which generally shows the development of a → *protagonist* from childhood to maturity.

**Biographical Criticism**, 90: → *author-oriented approach* in → *literary criticism*. It tries to establish a relation between the biography of an author and his or her works.

**book review**, 100: critical evaluation or discussion of book-length → *primary* or → *secondary sources* in a → *journal* or newspaper.

**camera angle**, 62: position of the camera or → *frame* in relation to an object that is represented; it is possible to distinguish between *high angle*, *straight-on angle* or *low angle* depending on the position of the camera.

**camera movement**, 62: early feature of → *film* that coincides with the development of lighter camera equipment, thus enabling the medium to abandon the static perspective of the → *proscenium stage*.

**canon**, 97: term originally used for holy → *texts*. It now refers to the entirety of those literary texts which are considered to be the most important in → *literary history*.

**catharsis**, 44: Greek: "cleansing"; term from Aristotle's theory of → *drama*. It argues that → *tragedy* has a cleansing and purging effect on the viewer.

**character**, 17–21: figure presented in a literary → *text*, including *main character* or → *protagonist* and → *minor character*. Recurring character types in drama are called → *stock characters*.

**characterization**, 19: the figures in a literary text can either be characterized as *types* or *individuals*. Types that show only one dominant feature are called → *flat characters*. If a figure is more complex, the term → *round character* is applied. In both cases, a figure has to be presented either through → *showing* (dramatic method) or → *telling* (narration); see also → *modes of presentation*.

**chiasmus**, 38: arrangement of letters, words and phrases in the form of a cross (from the Greek letter "X"); it is most commonly used in two adjacent lines of a poem.

**chorus**, 55: in classical → *Greek theater* the *chorus*, a group of reciters or chanters, was positioned in the orchestra between the audience and the → *actors*. Early Greek drama did not depend on → *dialogue* between the figures of a play as much as on dialogue between figures and the *chorus*. The *chorus* generally recited lyrical poems, either commenting on the action of the play or addressing the actors in a didactic manner.

**climax**, 15: also called *crisis* or *turning point*; crucial element of traditional → *plot* when the action undergoes decisive changes. In linear plots the climax is preceded by → *exposition* and → *complication* and followed by the → *resolution*.

**close reading**, 86: central term in → *New Criticism*. It is often used as a synonym for intrinsic or text immanent interpretation; see also → *affective fallacy* and → *intentional fallacy*.

**closet drama**, 46: stylized sub-genre of → *drama* which is not intended to be performed but to be read in private.

**collection of essays** or **anthology**, 6: collection of → *secondary sources* (→ *articles*) on specific topics compiled by one or several editors. If the anthology is published in honor of a well-known scholar, it is also referred to as a → *festschrift*.

**comedy**, 44: sub-genre of → *drama* with witty, humorous themes intended to entertain the audience. It is often regarded as the stylized continuation of primitive regeneration cults, such as the symbolic expulsion of winter by spring. This fertility symbolism culminates in the form of weddings as standard happy endings of traditional comedies.

**Comedy of Manners** or **Restoration Comedy**, 45: popular form of English → *drama* in the second half of seventeenth century, mainly portraying citizens from the upper ranks of society in witty → *dialogues*.

**complication** or conflict, 15: element of traditional → *plot*. During the complication, the initial → *exposition* is changed in order to develop into a → *climax*; in linear plots, it is preceded by the → *exposition* and followed by the → *climax*.

**concrete poetry**, 31: movement in → *poetry* focusing especially on the outward visual form of a poem, including shape and layout of letters, lines and → *stanzas*.

**context-oriented approaches**, 94–100: various movements and schools which approach a literary → *text* not merely as an intrinsic, independent work of art, but as part of a wider context. The context can be historical (e.g., → *New Historicism*), national (e.g., → *literary history*), socio-political (e.g., → *Marxist literary criticism*), generic (e.g., poetics) or gender-related (e.g., → *Feminist Literary Theory*).

**couplet**, 42: → *stanza* form that consists of two lines.

**critical apparatus**, 6, 113: formal element of → *secondary sources* which encompasses → *footnotes* or endnotes, a → *bibliography* (or list of works cited) and possibly an *index* of key words, names or titles.

**Cultural Studies**, 78: movement in the 1990s which is interested in culture as a comprehensive discourse-based phenomenon and thus shows striking structural analogies to trends in → *Deconstruction* and → *New Historicism*.

**dactyl**; 40: → *foot* in which a stressed syllable is followed by two unstressed syllables ( ´ ˘ ˘ ), as for example in "Júst fŏr ă | hándfŭl ŏf | sílvĕr hĕ | léft ŭs".

**Deconstruction**, 87–90: one of the most recent and complex movements of → *text-oriented approaches*, based on the works of the French philosopher Jacques Derrida (\*1930); like → *Semiotics*, it regards → *texts* as systems of → *signs*, but differs from traditional schools of → *Structuralism* by concentrating on the interaction of the → *signifiers*, almost abandoning the concept of a → *signified*; see also → *Poststructuralism*.

**defamiliarization**, 83: stylistic device, used to make the reader aware of literary conventions; related to the Brechtean *alienation effect*; see also → *metafiction*.

**denouement**, 15: French term for *resolution*, the last element of a linear → *plot* in which the → *complication* of the action is resolved after the → *climax*.

**detective novel**, 13: sub-genre of the → *novel* that centers around uncovering a crime.

**directing**, 49: level of → *transformation* between the → *text* and the → *performance* of → *drama* and → *film*. It includes conceptual steps which are not directly accessible for the audience but determine the performance and involve the choice of the script, casting, accentuation of the play, props, lighting, scenery, and rehearsals.

**discourse**, 4: term referring to oral or written expression within a certain thematic framework, as for example, historical, economic, political or feminist discourse; see also → *genre* and → *text type*.

**drama**, 44–56: one of the three classical literary → *genres*, involving the levels of → *text*, → *transformation* and → *performance*. Besides the written word, drama also relies on aspects of the → *performing arts*, including a number of non-verbal means of expression mainly of a visual kind, such as stage design, scenery, facial expressions, gestures, make-up, props and → *lighting*.

**editing**, 63: one of the final processes in the production of a → *film* when the various shots are cut and rearranged in a particular sequence; see also → *montage*.

**Eighteenth Century**, 70: period also known as the *Neoclassical, Golden* or *Augustan Age*. It brought major innovations and changes in English literature due to the introduction of newspapers and literary magazines as well as the evolution of the → *novel* and the → *essay* as new → *genres*.

**elegy**, 30: classical form of → *lyric poetry*. Its main theme is the lament for a deceased person.

**Elizabethan Age**, 69: period in English history, culture and → *literature* during the reign of Queen Elizabeth I (1558–1603); the term is sometimes used synonymously with → *Renaissance*.

**Elizabethan Theater**, 51: period of renewal for → *drama* in the English → *Renaissance* under the reign of Queen Elizabeth I (1558–1603); William Shakespeare (1564–1616) and Christopher Marlowe (1564–93) are among its most important representatives.

**end rhyme**, 41: → *rhyme* scheme based on identical syllables at the end of certain lines of a poem.

**English** or **Shakespearean Sonnet**, 42: the traditional → *sonnet* form in English literature, which consists of three → *quatrains* and one → *couplet* and uses iambic pentameter as its meter; its fourteen lines follow the → *rhyme* pattern *abab cdcd efef gg*.

**epic**, 10: long and complex form of → *narrative poetry*. It differs drastically from → *lyric poetry* in length, narrative technique, portrayal of → *characters* and → *plot*. At the centre of a complex plot stands a national hero who has to prove himself in numerous adventures and endure trials of cosmic dimensions. In the modern age, the epic has been overshadowed by the → *novel*; see also → *romance*.

**epistolary novel**, 12: sub-genre of the → *novel* which relates the → *plot* in → *first person narration* using letters of correspondence as its medium.

**essay**, 5: semi-literary → *genre*; popular in the seventeenth and eighteenth centuries. It deals with a particular topic in a scholarly manner while at the same time using a literary style. From the current perspective in → *literary criticism*, the *literary essay* can be classified as both → *primary* and → *secondary literature*. Today, the term *essay* is also used synonymously with → *article*.

**exposition**, 15: first element of a linear → *plot* when the initial situation of the enfolding action is revealed; in a linear plot, the *exposition* is followed by the → *complication*, the → *climax* and the → *denouement*.

**Expressionism**, 53: movement in various fields of art and → *literature* in the early twentieth century. It is characterized by the exaggeration of certain aspects of the "object" portrayed (e.g. strong lines in painting or the emphasis on types in the characterization of figures in literature); it is often seen as a counter-movement or reaction to → *Realism*.

**external method**, 55: one of the two major methods in → *actor* training. Its goal is the actor's imitation of moods required by a role through the use of certain techniques, rather than through actually feeling these moods. This approach, which goes back to Konstantin Stanislavsky (1863–1938) and his pupil Lee Strasberg (1901–82), is also referred to as *The Method* and stands in contrast to the → *internal method* that is based on the personal emotional involvement of the actor.

**eye rhyme**, 42: type of → *rhyme* which is based on syllables with identical spelling but different pronunciation.

**Feminist Literary Theory**, 97–99: encompasses recent → *context-oriented approaches* whose different methodologies focus on gender as a starting point for literary analysis; see also → *Gender Theory*.

**Festschrift**, 5: → *collection of essays* in honor of a distinguished scholar; see also → *anthology* and → *secondary source*.

**fiction**, 10–28: term to differentiate the literary prose genres of → *short story*, → *novella* and → *novel* from → *drama* and → *poetry*; in older → *secondary sources* it is often used synonymously with → *epic*.

**figural narrative situation**, 21, 23: → *point of view* in which the narrator moves into the background, suggesting that the → *plot* is revealed solely through the actions of the → *characters* in the → *text*. This technique is a relatively recent phenomenon that developed with the rise of the modern → *novel*, mostly as a means of encouraging the reader to judge the action without an intervening commentator.

**film**, 56–66: in spite of different means of expression, → *drama* and film are often summarized under the heading → *performing arts* because of their use of → *actors*. From a formalist-structuralist perspective, however, film seems closer to the → *novel* than to drama because of its "fixed" (i.e. recorded) character; see also → *spatial*, → *temporal*, and → *acoustic dimension of film*.

**film stock**, 61: the raw material onto which individual → *frames* are photographed. The deliberate use of black and white or color, high or low contrast film stock produces structural effects which indirectly influence levels of content; see also → *spatial dimension of film*.

**first person narration**, 22: → *point of view* in which one of the → *characters* who is part of the → *plot* tells the story, referring to her- or himself in the first person singular.

**flashback**, 63: device in the structuring of → *plot* which introduces events from the past in an otherwise linear narrative; see also → *foreshadowing*.

**flat character**, 17: in contrast to → *round characters*, this kind of figure displays only one dominant character trait; see also → *characterization*.

**foot**, 40: according to the sequence of stressed and unstressed syllables, it is possible to distinguish four important metrical feet: 1 → *iambus*: an unstressed syllable followed by a stressed syllable ( ˘´ ); 2 → *anapest*: two unstressed syllables followed by a stressed syllable ( ˘˘´ ); 3 → *trochee*: a stressed syllable followed by an unstressed syllable ( ´˘ ); 4 → *dactyl*: a stressed syllable is followed by two unstressed syllables ( ´˘˘ ).

**footnote** or endnote, 114: references to → *primary* or → *secondary sources*, or additional commentary, either as a *footnote* at the bottom of the page or as an *endnote* at the end of a research paper.

**foreshadowing**, 15: device in the structuring of → *plot* which brings information from the future into the current action; see also → *flashback*.

**Formalism**, 81–85: term that is mostly used synonymously with → *Structuralism* to characterize → *text-oriented approaches* in the first half of the twentieth century which focused on the formal aspects of a literary work; see also → *Russian Formalism*.

**frame**, 61: segment of a scene, person or object represented on → *film*. It is closely connected to terms such as *close-up*, *medium* and *long shot* that refer to the distance between the camera and the filmed object or person, as well as to the choice of which segment of a setting is to be represented. Similar effects can be achieved with wide-angle or telephoto lenses; see also → *mise-en-scène*.

**Gender Theory**, 97–99: recent development of → *Feminist Literary Theory* that no longer focuses exclusively on women, but tries to include issues concerning both genders in the → *interpretation* of literary → *texts*.

**genre**, 3–4: term to classify the traditional literary forms of → *epic* (i.e. → *fiction*), → *drama* and → *poetry*. These categories or genres are still commonly used, although the epic has been replaced by the → *novel* and → *short story*. In the English-speaking world, genre denotes *fiction, drama* and *poetry*; see also → *discourse* and → *text type*.

**gothic novel**, 13: sub-genre of the → *novel* with an eerie, supernatural → *setting*. It was particularly popular in the nineteenth century.

**Greek theater**, 51: open-air amphitheater consisting of an *orchestra* and a *skene* (stage building). The audience was seated in circles around the orchestra. The → *actors* moved between the *skene* and the *orchestra*, and the → *chorus* was positioned in the *orchestra* between the audience and the actors. In the comedies and tragedies of classical Greek drama, all actors wore masks.

**hermeneutics**, 77: traditional term for scholarly → *interpretation* of a → *text*.

**historical novel**, 12: sub-genre of the → *novel* with → *characters* and → *plot* in a realistic-historical context. New Journalism, which recounts real events in the form of a novel, is a related movement in the second half of the twentieth century.

**history play**, 45: sub-genre of → *drama*. In the English tradition, it dates back to the → *Renaissance* and dramatizes historical events or personalities.

**iambus**, 40: → *foot* in which an unstressed syllable is followed by a stressed syllable ( ˘ ´ ), as for example, in "Thĕ cúr| fĕw tólls | thĕ knéll | ŏf pár | tĭng dáy").

**imagery**, 30: term which derives from the Latin "imago" ("picture"), and refers mainly to the use of concrete language to lend a visual quality to abstract themes in a poem; see also → *Imagism*.

**Imagism**, 35: literary movement in the early twentieth century closely associated with Ezra Pound. It attempts to reduce and condense → *poetry* to essential "images." Concrete language without decorative elements is employed to achieve a strong visual effect or → *imagery*.

**individualization**, 19: → *characterization* that emphasizes a multiplicity of character traits in a literary figure, rather than one dominant feature; see also → *typification*.

**intentional fallacy**, 86: "wrong belief in the author's intention"; important term of → *New Criticism*, aimed against → *interpretations* which try to reconstruct the author's original intentions when writing a → *text* and which thereby neglects intrinsic aspects of the text; see also → *affective fallacy*.

**interior monologue**, 24: narrative technique in which a figure is exclusively characterized by his or her thoughts without any other comments; it is influenced by psychoanalysis and related to the → *stream-of-consciousness technique*.

**internal method**, 55: one of the two main methods in → *actor* training. It builds on individual identification of the actor with her or his part. In contrast to the → *external method*, which tries to simulate personal feelings, this method works with the internalization of emotions and situations that are required in the part.

**internal rhyme**, 41: type of → *rhyme* which is not based on → *end rhyme* but rather → *alliteration* or → *assonance*; most → *Old English* and some → *Middle English* → *poetry* uses internal rhyme.

**interpretation**, 77: modern term for → *hermeneutics* and *exegesis*, i.e., the search for the meaning of a → *text*; often seen in opposition to evaluative → *literary criticism*.

**journal**, 5: regularly issued scholarly publication which contains → *essays* and sometimes → *notes*, → *book reviews* or → *review essays*; see also → *secondary source*.

**lighting**, 61: visual element used in → *film* and → *drama* to enhance levels of content visually.

**literary criticism**, 100: systematic, scholarly approach to literary → *texts*, often used synonymously with → *interpretation*; see also → *literary theory*.

**Literary History**, 94 → *context-oriented approach* which mainly deals with the chronological and periodical classification of literary → *texts*. This movement is informed by historical methodology; it dates and categorizes literary works and examines the influence of earlier on later works.

**Literary Theory**, 77: also referred to as *Critical Theory*; philosophical and methodological basis of → *literary criticism*, including varying approaches to texts; the respective schools can be grouped according to → *text-*, → *author-*, → *reader-* and → *context-oriented approaches*.

**literature**, 1–7: vague umbrella term for written expression; it conventionally refers to → *primary* and → *secondary sources;* see also → *text*.

**lyric poetry**, 29: term for a variety of short poetic forms such as the → *sonnet*, the → *ode* and the → *elegy*. In contrast to the more complex and longer → *narrative poetry*, it usually revolves around a single event, impression or idea.

**Marxist Literary Theory**, 95: → *context-oriented approach* based on the writings of Karl Marx (1818–83) and other Marxist theorists. It analyzes literary → *texts* as expressions of economic, sociological and political backgrounds. Conditions of production in particular periods are examined with respect to their influence on literary writings of the time.

**metafiction**, 83: "writing about writing"; term for self-reflexive literary → *texts* which focus on their own literary elements, such as language, narrative and → *plot* structure; it is a main feature of → *Postmodernism*.

**metaphor**, 33: → *rhetorical figure* which "equates" one thing with another without actually "comparing" the two (e.g., "My love is a red, red rose"); see also → *simile*.

**meter**, 39: element of the → *acoustic-rhythmical dimension* of → *poetry*; stressed and unstressed syllables of a line can be organized in → *feet*. In order to describe the meter of a verse, one indicates the name of the foot and the number of the feet used (e.g., iambic pentameter = 5 iambuses in each verse).

**Middle English Period**, 69: period of linguistic and → *literary history*. It is considered to begin with the invasion of England by the French-speaking Normans in the eleventh century and ends with the advent of the Renaissance at the end of the fifteenth century; dominant literary genres are the → *romance* and the *tale*.

**minor character**, 23: figure in a literary → *text* who – in contrast to the → *protagonist* – does not occupy the center of attention.

**"minority" literatures**, 73: problematic umbrella term for movements in → *literature* toward the end of the twentieth century which are represented by marginalized gender groups (women, gays, and lesbians) and ethnic groups (African Americans, Chicanos and Chicanas, etc.).

**Mis-en-scène**, 61: French for "to place on stage"; the term refers to the arrangement of all visual elements in a theater production. In film it is used as an umbrella term for the various elements that constitute the frame, including camera distance, camera angles, lenses, lighting, as well as the positioning of persons and objects in relation to each other; see also → *frame*.

**Modernism**, 72: period of literary and cultural history in the first decades of the twentieth century. It can be seen as a reaction to the realist tendencies of the late nineteenth century. New narrative structures, → *points of view* (e.g., → *stream of consciousness technique*) and other literary forms of expression are introduced under the influence of visual art and psychoanalysis.

**modes of presentation**, 20: as concerns the presentation of → *characters* and events in a literary work, it is possible to distinguish between *explanatory characterization* based on *narration* (→ *telling*) and *dramatic characterization* based on → *dialogues* and → *monologues* (→ *showing*).

**monograph**, 5: scholarly or book-length publication on a specific topic, → *text* or author; see also → *secondary source*.

**monologue** or **soliloquy**, 47: long speech on stage which is not aimed at a direct → *dialogue* partner. In the → *aside*, a special form of monologue, a character on stage passes on information to the audience which is not accessible to the other figures in the play.

**montage**, 63: → *editing* technique in → *film*. Its effects resemble those of → *rhetorical figures* in → *literature* (e.g., metaphorical meaning): by combining two different images, the meaning of one object can be associated with the other, as occurs in the relationship between *tenor* and *vehicle* in → *metaphor*. Montage is closely associated with the innovations of the Russian filmmaker Sergei Eisenstein (1898–1948).

**mystery** and **miracle play**, 44: medieval dramatic forms in which religious-allegorical or biblical themes were adapted to be performed outside the church; together with the classical Latin drama, they influenced the revival of → *drama* in the → *Renaissance*.

**myth criticism**, 84: approach which investigates the mythological deep-structures of literary → *texts* and uses them as a basis for → *interpretation*; see also → *Archetypal Criticism*.

**narrative poetry**, 29: in contrast to the shorter and more focused → *lyric poetry*, it includes → *genres* such as the → *epic*, the → *romance* and the → *ballad*, which tell a story with a clearly defined plot.

**Naturalism**, 71: term denoting → *texts* from the end of the nineteenth century which aim at a realistic depiction of the influence of social and environmental circumstances on → *characters* in literary texts; see also → *Realism*.

**New Criticism**, 85–87: one of the most important Anglo-American → *text-oriented approaches* in the decades after World War II; it differentiates → *interpretation* from source studies, socio-historical background studies, history of motifs, as well as → *author-oriented* biographical or → *psychoanalytical approaches* and → *reception history* in order to free → *literary criticism* from extrinsic elements – i.e., those outside the text – and bring the focus back to the literary text as such; see also → *Structuralism*; → *affective* fallacy,→ *intentional fallacy* and → *close reading*.

**New Historicism**, 95–96: recent → *context-oriented approach* which builds on → *Poststructuralism* and → *Deconstruction* but also includes historical dimensions in the discussion of literary → *texts*, presupposing a structural similarity between literary and other → *discourses* within a given historical period.

**note**, 5: short → *secondary source* in a scholarly → *journal*. It treats a very specific aspect of a topic in only a few paragraphs.

**novel**, 11–13: important → *genre* of prose → *fiction* which developed in England in the eighteenth century; the → *epic* and the → *romance* are indirect precursors. Structurally, the novel differs from the epic through more complex → *character presentation* and → *point of view* techniques, its emphasis on → *realism*, and a more subtle structuring of the → *plot*.

**novella** or **novelette**, 14: sub-genre of prose → *fiction*. Due to its shortness and idiosyncratic narrative elements, it assumes a position between the → *short story* and the → *novel*.

**ode**, 30: traditional form of → *lyric poetry* on a serious, mostly classical theme and consisting of several → *stanzas*.

**Old English** or **Anglo-Saxon Period**, 68: earliest period of English literature and language between the invasion of Britain by Germanic

tribes (Angles, Saxons, Jutes) in the 5th century AD and the con
quest of England by William the Conqueror in 1066; the mos
important → *genres* are the → *epic* and → *poetry* (including *charms* an
*riddles*).

**omniscient point of view**, 21: → *point of view* which describes the action
from an omniscient, God-like perspective by referring to the → *protag
onist* in the third person. It is therefore often imprecisely termed *thir
person narration*.

**onomatopoeia**, 30: linguistic term for a word which resembles the soun
produced by the object it denotes (e.g., "cuckoo"); in → *poetry*, i
attempts to emphasize the meaning of a word through its acousti
dimension.

**paraphrase**, 114: summary in one's own words of a passage from a →
*secondary* or → *primary source*; see also → *quotation*.

**performance**, 54–56: last phase in the → *transformation* of a dramatic →
*text* into a staged play; see also → *drama* and → *actor*.

**performing arts**; 57: umbrella term for artistic expressions that cente
around the → *performance* of an → *actor* in a stage-like setting; see als
→ *drama* and → *film*.

**Philology**, 79–80: summarizes an approach in traditional → *literary criticism
It deals especially with "material" aspects of → *texts*, such as th
editing of manuscripts, the preservation and reconstruction of texts

**picaresque novel**, 12: sub-genre of the → *novel*. It recounts the episodi
adventures of a vagrant rogue (Spanish: "picaro") who usually get
into trouble by breaking social norms; it attempts to expose socia
injustice in a satirical way.

**plot**, 15–17: logical combination of different elements of the action in a
literary → *text*. In an ideal linear plot, the initial situation or → *expo
sition* is followed by a → *complication* or conflict which creates suspens
and then leads to a → *climax*, crisis or turning point. The climax i
then followed by the resolution or → *denouement*, which usually mark
the end of a text.

**poetry** or **poem**, 28–44: literary → *genre* which differs from prose → *genre
in the use of verse, → *rhyme*, and → *meter*. In modern prose poem
or experimental poetry, these classical elements are no longer valid
however, the wording and the deliberate use of certain structura
elements of syntax and → *rhetorical figures* mark these works as poeti
forms; see also → *narrative poetry* and → *lyric poetry*.

**point of view** or **narrative perspective**, 21–25: the way in which →
*characters*, events and → *settings* in a → *text* are presented. Narratolog
distinguishes between three basic points of view: the action of a tex
is either mediated through an exterior unspecified narrator (→ *omni
scient point of view*), through a person involved in the action (→ *firs
person narration*), or presented without additional commentary throug

the acting figures (→ *figural narrative situation*); see also → *stream-of-consciousness technique*.

**Postcolonial Literature**, 73: umbrella term that refers to → *texts* from former British territories in the Caribbean, Africa, India and Australia which have attracted the attention of contemporary literary critics. Sometimes also referred to as *New Literatures in English, Commonwealth Literatures* and *Anglophone Literatures*.

**Postmodernism**, 72: movement in literary and cultural history in the second half of the twentieth century which takes up issues which were treated by → *Modernism* – e.g., innovative narrative techniques and → *plot* patterns – by dealing with them on an academic, often formal level; see also → *metafiction*.

**Poststructuralism**, 82: umbrella term for the → *text-oriented* schools in literary theory in the second half of the twentieth century, such as → *Semiotics* and → *Deconstruction*, which go beyond the traditional schools of → *Structuralism* and → *Formalism*.

**primary source**, 5: term for literary → *texts*, usually belonging to the three traditional → *genres*; see also → *secondary source*.

**proscenium stage**, 53: dominant → *stage* form since the Baroque. Because of its box-like shape, it was the preferred stage for Realist drama.

**protagonist**, 22: technical term for the main → *character* in a literary → *text*; see also → *minor character*.

**Psychoanalytic Literary Criticism**, 92: movement in → *literary criticism* which applies the methods of Sigmund Freud's (1856–1939) psychoanalysis; psychological traits of the author are examined in the → *text* and literary → *characters* are analyzed as if they were real people; see also → *archetypal criticism*.

**Puritan Age**, 70: religiously motivated movement which dominated English culture from 1649 to 1660; the term is also used for the Colonial Period in the seventeenth and eighteenth centuries as the first literary movement on the North American continent.

**quatrain**, 42: → *stanza* that consists of four lines.

**quotation**, 114: passage which has been directly taken from a → *primary* or → *secondary source*; see also → *paraphrase*.

**reader-oriented approach**, 92–94: school in → *literary criticism* in the second half of the twentieth century. It concentrates on the relation between → *text* and reader. The most important movements are → *reception theory, reader-response theory, reception-aesthetic* and → *reception history*.

**Realism**, 71: term for the period in → *literary history* toward the end of the nineteenth century which was preoccupied with translating "reality" into → *literature*; it is also used as a general term for realistic portrayal in literature; see also → *Naturalism*.

**reception history**, 94: → *reader-oriented approach* which deals with the reception of a → *text* by the reader; sales figures, critical statements and reviews from magazines and scholarly → *journals* provide data for a *synchronic* analysis (i.e., one taking place within a certain period) of readers' reactions, as well as a *diachronic* analysis (i.e., one which compares historical periods) of the reception of texts.

**Reception Theory**, 92: also *reception aesthetic* or *reader-response theory*; movement in the interpretation of texts which focuses primarily on the reader; it stands in contrast to intrinsic or → *text-oriented approaches*; see also → *reception history*.

**Renaissance**, 69: period in English literary and cultural history which traditionally encompasses the sixteenth and parts of the seventeenth centuries; it is often subdivided into periods named after the rulers of the time, such as the → *Elizabethan* Age (for Queen Elizabeth I ) or Jacobean Age (for King James). The classical → *genre* of → *drama* experiences its first revival in English → *literature*; linguistics often applies the term *Early Modern Period*.

**restoration comedy**, 45: see → *comedy of manners*.

**review article**, 100: longer form of the → *book review*. It discusses a number of pieces of → *secondary literature* on a common topic.

**Rhetoric**, 80–81: precursor of modern → *text-oriented approaches* which dates back to the practice of oratory in classical antiquity. As a source of rules for good public speech, it contains detailed instructions for every phase of oratory: *inventio* (finding themes), *dispositio* (structuring material), *elocutio* (wording with the aid of rhetorical figures), *memoria* (techniques for remembering the speech) and *actio* (delivery of the speech).

**rhetorical figures** or **figures of speech**, 33: a number of stylistic forms which mostly use language in its "non-literal" meaning; see → *metaphor*, → *simile*, → *symbol*.

**rhyme** or **rime**, 41: element of → *rhythmic-acoustic dimension* of a poem. In English, it generally includes → *internal rhymes* (based on → *alliteration* and → *assonance)*, → *end rhymes* (the most frequent kind of rhyme in modern poems, based on identical syllables at the end of certain lines) and the → *eye rhymes* (which play with identical spelling but different pronunciation of words and syllables).

**rhythmic-acoustic dimension**, 38–44: umbrella term for elements of → *poetry* such as *sound*, → *rhyme*, → *meter*, and → *onomatopoeia*.

**romance**, 10: most classical romances were written in prose, most medieval ones in verse. Because of its advanced use of → *point of view* and the structuring of → *plot*, the romance is regarded as the first direct precursor of the → *novel*, despite its verse form. In contrast to the → *epic*, the romance is more focused in terms of plot and less concerned with cosmic or national issues.

**Romanticism**, 70: movement in → *literary history* in the first half of the nineteenth century. It appears more or less simultaneously in American and English literature. Nature → *poetry* and individual, emotional experiences play important roles. Romanticism may be seen as a reaction to the Enlightenment and the political changes throughout Europe and America at the end of the eighteenth century. In America, Romanticism partly overlaps with → *Transcendentalism*.

**round character**, 17: figure which is characterized through a number of different character traits; see also → *flat character* and → *characterization*.

**Russian Formalism**, 82: → *text-oriented approach* developed during and after World War I. It was interested in the nature of literary language and is famous for the concept of → *defamiliarization*; see also → *Structuralism*.

**satirical novel**, 12: sub-genre of the → *novel*. It points out the weaknesses of society by exaggerating social conventions.

**scene**, 48: subdivision of → *acts* in traditional → *drama*, and therefore the smallest unit in the overall structure of a play.

**secondary source**, 5–7: scholarly → *text types* including → *notes*, → *essays*, → reviews, and → *monographs* that usually deal with → *primary sources*.

**Semiotics**, 87–90: one of the recent → *text-oriented approaches* which defines the → *text* as an interdependent network of → *signs*. It expands the notion of text to include non-verbal systems of signs, such as → *film*, painting, fashion, geography, etc. The basis for this complex theory is the concept of language of the Swiss linguist Ferdinand de Saussure (1857–1913) which is based on the terms → *signifier* and → *signified*; see also → *Deconstruction* and → *Poststructuralism*.

**setting**, 25–28: dimension of literary → *texts* including the time and place of the action. The setting is usually carefully chosen by the author in order to support indirectly → *plot*, → *characters*, and → *point of view*.

**short story**, 13–15: short → *genre* of prose → *fiction* that is related to fairy tales and myths. Medieval and early modern cycles of narratives are indirect models. Formally, the short story generally differs from the → *novel* in size, in its less complex → *plot* and → *setting*, in its less differentiated → *characterization* of figures and in its less complex use of → *point of view*.

**showing**, 19: → *mode of presentation* which, in contrast to narration or → *telling*, relies on dramatic presentation (e.g., direct speech).

**sign**, 87: meaningful element within a closed system (e.g., → *text*); see also → *Semiotics*.

**signified**, 87, 88: the linguist Ferdinand de Saussure divided language into two basic dimensions: the mental concept (e.g., the idea of a tree), termed the *signified*; and that concept's manifestation in language (the sequence of sounds or letters in the word "T-R-E-E"), termed the *signifier*; see also → *Semiotics* and → *Deconstruction*.

**signifier**, 87, 88: see → *signified*.

**simile**, 33: → *rhetorical figure* which "compares" two different things by connecting them with "like," "than," "as," or "compare" (e.g., "Oh, my love is like a red, red rose"); see also → *metaphor*.

**soliloquy**, 47: see → *monologue*.

**sonnet**, 30: poem with a strict → *rhyme* scheme; it is often used for the treatment of "worldly love" in → *poetry*; according to the rhyme scheme and the kind of → *stanza* it is possible to distinguish between → *English or Shakespearean*, Spenserian, Italian and Petrarchan sonnets.

**spatial dimension of film**, 61–63: umbrella term for a number of heterogeneous aspects in film, such as → *film stock*, → *lighting*, → *camera angle*, → *camera movement*, → *point of view*, → *editing*, and → *montage*; see also → *mise-en-scène*.

**stage**, 51–56: the various designs of theater stages can be reduced to the two basic types of the → *amphitheater* and the → *proscenium stage*; most other common forms combine elements of these two.

**stanza**, 42: element of the visual dimension of a poem which can be classified according to the number of its lines, their meter and rhyme; most poems are a combination of the → *couplet* (2 lines), → *tercet* (3 lines) and → *quatrain* (4 lines); see also → *sonnet*.

**stock character**, 55: recurring → *flat character* in → *drama*, such as the boastful soldier, the cranky old man or the crafty servant.

**stream-of-consciousness technique**, 24: narratological technique (related to → *interior monologue*) which is used to represent the subconscious associations of a fictitious persona. It reflects a groundbreaking shift in cultural paradigms during the first decades of the twentieth century; the most famous example is the final section of James Joyce's novel *Ulysses* (1922).

**Structuralism**, 81–85: umbrella term for → *text-oriented approaches* which use formal-structural aspects (intrinsic approach) in the → *interpretation* of → *texts* and neglect historical, sociological, biographical and psychological dimensions; the most important schools are → *Russian Formalism* and the *Prague School of Structuralism* in the first half of the twentieth century. In the Anglo-American context, → *New Criticism* developed as a related movement; see also → *Semiotics* and → *Deconstruction*.

**stylistics**, 80–81: → *text-oriented approach* for the description of stylistic idiosyncrasies of authors, texts or national literatures; it deals with grammatical structures (vocabulary, syntax), elements of sound (phonology), and over-arching forms (→ *rhetorical figures*) of → *texts*.

**symbol**, 33: term for "objects" in a literary text which transcend their material meaning; it is possible to distinguish between *conventional symbols* (which are commonly known) and *private symbols* (which are created by an author for a particular text).

**telling**, 19: one of the two basic → *modes of presentation* in literary → *texts*. In contrast to the → *showing*, it relies mostly on narration.

**temporal dimension of film**, 63–66: includes aspects such as slow-motion, fast motion, plot time, length of film, → *flashback* and → *foreshadowing*.

**tercet**, 42: → *stanza* that consists of three lines.

**text**, 1–7: term often used synonymously with → *literature*; in recent usage, it is also applied to denote non-verbal → *sign* systems such as fashion, → *film*, geography, painting; see also → *Semiotics* and → *Deconstruction*.

**text-oriented approaches**, 79–90: movements or schools in → *literary theory* which concentrate on the "textual" or intrinsic levels of literature by deliberately excluding extrinsic aspects – i.e., those external to the text – concerning the author (biography, complete works), audience (class, gender, age, ethnic origin, education) or context (historical, social or political conditions). The *text-oriented approaches* include → *Philology*, → *Rhetoric* and → *Stylistics*, as well as the formalist-structuralist schools of → *Russian Formalism, Prague School of Structuralism*, → *New Criticism*, → *Semiotics* and → *Deconstruction*.

**text type**, 3–4: linguistic term used for the classification of forms of expression which are mostly written, but which are not necessarily of a literary kind. It includes → *primary* and → *secondary sources*, → *texts* of everyday use, advertisements, instruction manuals, etc.; see also → *genre* and → *discourse*.

**Theater of the Absurd**, 53: movement in twentieth century → *drama* which abandons traditional → *plot* structures and conventional → *character presentation* in favor of new modes of portraying the disillusioned human condition after World War II.

**three unities**, 47: rules concerning the unity of place, time and action in → *drama*, deriving from (mis)interpretations of Aristotle's works in the → *Renaissance* which argue that, in a "good" play, the place of the action should not change, the time of the → *plot* presented should correspond more or less with the length of the → *performance*, and the action should follow a linear → *plot*.

**tragedy**, 44: classical sub-genre of → *drama* with serious themes, usually depicting the downfall of an important figure, intended to have a purging effect on the audience; see also → *catharsis*.

**Transcendentalism**, 71: period in the first half of the nineteenth century in the Unites States. It became the most important uniquely American literary movement; it was partly influenced by Romantic enthusiasm for nature and German Idealism.

**transformation**, 49–54: link between the textual dimension and → *performance* in → *drama*. It primarily revolves around → *directing*.

**trochee**, 40: → *foot* in which a stressed syllable is followed by an unstressed syllable ( ˊ˘ ), as for example in "Thére thĕy | áre, mў | fiftў | mén ănd | wómĕn").

**type**, 17: see → *flat character*.

**typification**, 17: typified → *characters* diplay one dominant feature which often represents an abstract idea or the general traits of a group of persons. Medieval allegorical depictions of figures preferred *typification* in order to personify vices, virtues, or philosophical and religious positions; see also → *individualization*.

**utopian novel**, 12: sub-genre of the → *novel* describing alternative worlds with the aim of revealing and criticizing existing socio-political conditions.

# Notes

1   Kurt Vonnegut, *Slaughterhouse-Five* (1969; London: Cape, 1970) 76.

2   Mark Twain, "A True Story," *The Writings of Mark Twain*, vol. 19 (New York, London: Harper & Brothers Publishers, 1903) 265–72.

3   Charlotte Brontë, *Jane Eyre* (1847; Rutland: J.M. Dent & Sons Ltd, 1991) 126.

4   Ernest Hemingway, "The Short Happy Life of Francis Macomber," *The Complete Short Stories of Ernest Hemingway* (New York: Charles Scribner's Sons, 1987) 5–28.

5   This simplified structure roughly follows Franz K. Stanzel, *Typische Formen des Romans*, 12th edn. (Göttingen: Vandenhoeck & Ruprecht, 1993), which was later expanded and revised in *A Theory of Narrative*, trans. Charlotte Goedsche (Cambridge: Cambridge University Press, 1984). Recent narratology, however, has produced a large number of competing models using patterns different from Stanzel's triade. For a helpful and very concise survey of theoretical positions in contemporary narratology see Manfred Jahn and Ansgar Nünning, "A Survey of Narratological Models," *Literatur in Wissenschaft und Unterricht* 27.4 (1994) 283–303.

6　　Jane Austen, *Northanger Abbey* (1818; London: Virago, 1989) 9.

7　　J.D. Salinger, *The Catcher in the Rye* (1951; Harmondsworth: Penguin, 1978) 1.

8　　James Joyce, *A Portrait of the Artist as a Young Man* (1916; Harmondsworth: Penguin, 1983) 58–9.

9　　Margaret Atwood, *The Edible Woman* (1969; New York: Bantam Books, 1991) 105.

10　　Edgar Allan Poe, "The Fall of the House of Usher," *The Complete Works of Edgar Allan Poe*, ed. James Harrison, vol. 3 (New York: AMS Press, 1965) 273–7.

11　　Virginia Woolf, *Mrs Dalloway* (1925; New York: Harcourt Brace Jovanovich, 1990) 3–5; my emphasis.

12　　*The Anglo-Saxon World*, ed. and trans. Kevin Crossley-Holland (Totowa: Barnes & Nobel Books, 1983) 243.

13　　*Mittelenglische Lyrik*, eds. Werner Arens und Rainer Schöwerling (Stuttgart: Reclam 1980) 88–9.

14　　W.H. Auden, *Collected Shorter Poems, 1927–1957* (New York: Random House, 1975) 92.

15　　Ezra Pound, "A Few Don'ts," *Poetry*, I (1913) 6; repr. in *Literary Essays of Ezra Pound*, ed. T.S. Eliot (Norfolk, CT: New Directions, n.d.) 4.

16　　Aristotle, *The Poetics*, trans. Hamilton Fyfe and W. Rhys Roberts (Cambridge: Harvard University Press, 1991) chapter 6.

17　　Quoted from Victor Erlich, *Russian Formalism: History – Doctrine* (New Haven, London: Yale University Press, 1981) 172.

18　　Umberto Eco, "Regretfully, We are Returning ... Reader's Reports" (1972), *Misreadings*, trans. William Weaver (San Diego, New York: Harcourt Brace & Company, 1993) 33.

19　　Joseph Gibaldi, *MLA Handbook for Writers of Research Papers*, 5th edn. (New York: The Modern Language Association, 1999).

# Author and title index

# Subject index